BUSINESS PROCESS MAPPING

BUSINESS PROCESS MAPPING

How to Improve Customer Experience and Increase Profitability in a Post-COVID World

SECOND EDITION

NAKATINDI CHALANSI

Project Management Resources by Nakatindi Chalansi

Free process templates are available for corporate strategy analysis, process hierarchies and levels, SWOT analysis, process rankings, RACI matrix, SIPOCs, customer journeys, and current and future state processes on the author's website: www.nakatindichalansi.com.

From September 2022, you will be able to find project and programme management resources on our website www.nakatindichalansi.com. The resource centre consists of books, ebooks and templates to download on business cases, business processes and business readiness guides.

High-level Contents

Detailed Contents

Chapter Five: Customer Journey Mapping Techniques   107

Chapter Six: Redefining the Customer Experience   127

Introduction

EVERY BUSINESS OPERATES like moving assembly lines or robotic carriers from one function to the next. Those strategic leaders who prioritise agile transformation, customer experience, process improvement, data analytics, artificial intelligence (AI), technology innovation, and a skilled workforce will always sustain dominance in the business landscape. It is now obvious that enterprises need more talented strategic teams and revolutionise their corporate strategies to compete in the ever-changing marketplace.

The impact of the COVID-19 crisis has changed customer habits and preferences. This shift in consumer demands has forced many companies to redefine their business processes and change how technology delivers value-adding products and services to their demanding customers through online and offline or face-to-face multi-dimensional shopping channels.

Is it because this rapid global change requires companies to apply the successful principles of high-performing organisations (HPOs)? An HPO is a business entity that surpasses the financial and non-financial performance of its competitors. This, for example, can include profitability, revenue, product design, customer satisfaction, technology innovation, processes, and many other metrics.

Characteristics of High-Performing Organisations

The HPOs seem to outperform their peers by drawing agile strategies with quicker responses to the desired changes, maximising technology, and maintaining business continuity in a global crisis. Other factors include streamlining business processes, optimising artificial intelligence, applying digitisation for seamless customer experience, creating new organisational design structures, maintaining a talented workforce, and supporting progressive ethical culture.

1

Characteristics of High-Performing Organisations (HPOs)

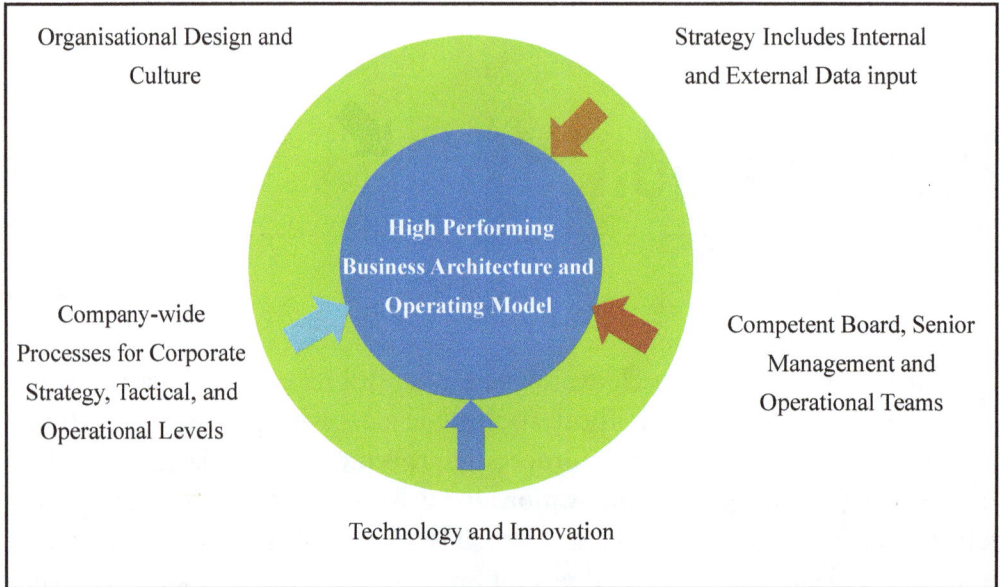

Organisational Design and Culture

Strategy Includes Internal and External Data input

High Performing Business Architecture and Operating Model

Company-wide Processes for Corporate Strategy, Tactical, and Operational Levels

Competent Board, Senior Management and Operational Teams

Technology and Innovation

Figure 1: *Operating Model for High-Performing Organisations (HPOs)*

The HPO status can be achieved by designing robust, and innovative business processes and operating models, elaborated in chapter two of this publication.

The focus is on eliminating the preconceived notion that business process value only relates to documenting detailed operational activities. This book throws light on how business processes can also serve as significant tools that can be used effectively to analyse strategic decisions at high level, thereby resulting in arriving at important decisions quickly without extensive detail. For example, this could be senior management teams requesting process information. Rather than depending exclusively on functional KPIs that are valuable, an alternate methodology can be identifying the processes that exist in each function, followed by outlining the complex ones, thus leading to the generation of maximum revenue, maximum customer satisfaction, and optimum operational costs. This can be a more exact assessment of the organisation's operational efficiency, consequently impacting the investment allocation decisions.

From business evaluations, you will find that business performance is significantly driven by process maximisation in business operating architecture. When you think about any global high-value business leading in their industry, you will learn that there is a high correlation between profitability and operational process management across the organisation.

This book talks about how to prioritise process optimisation for improving business performance. The approach can start from using process frameworks in framing your strategy, cascaded to tactical and operational levels in obtaining operational efficiencies in both short and long-term timescales.

Here are the critical processes that have been identified as great contributors to high-performing organisations (HPOs):

Corporate Strategy Processes

The corporate strategy process essentially defines the 'future' by visualising and creating strategic objectives to arrive at that future state. The predominant aim of any corporate strategy for a profit-making business is to improve the firm's performance and profitability of its investors, owners, and shareholders.

Business processes are essential components of corporate strategy because they connect various parts of the organisation and help define how each business function fits into the broader business plan. Corporate strategy success is often derived from process excellence while creating, defining, and evaluating, and during execution. An organisation's corporate strategy direction is formulated by strategic talent, strategic software, creativity and data science, including analysis performed to arrive at the values, purpose, mission, vision, and objectives. It is also a known fact that traditional corporate strategy processes are no longer effective because of the rapidly changing business environments. Chalking out suitable and agile corporate strategy processes is the key solution for an HPO to optimise and adapt to the immediate and/or significant changes more effectively.

"Corporate strategy is a complex process, particularly for global geographic segments that require different goals for their strategic environments. Many businesses spend an excessive amount of time planning the strategy while failing to provide sufficient resources to execute the company's strategy at all levels of the organisation" (*Source: BCG.com*). The goal is to create a balance between the time spent in corporate strategy creation, analysis, and execution.

New companies are constantly entering the market with different corporate strategy methodologies, frequently creating, monitoring, and adapting their company direction. Their strategies have agile frameworks for changing and discontinuing an objective if the actual results are not adding value to their expectations.

The new entrants' financial performance, non-financial performance, and forecasts are closely monitored for better strategic decision-making purposes after the corporate strategy has been agreed upon. There is, however, no hesitancy in changing the direction if the chosen objective is not delivering the desired results.

What exactly separates the best companies from their competitors? Some critical factors could start with their agile strategies, careful selection of product portfolios that generate profitable revenue streams, an innovative product design workforce, and brand strategies that understand what customers want. Customer satisfaction is the key to all decisions that are taken and giving the customers a consistently positive consumer experience is prioritised by optimising technology and process innovation.

Strategic Leadership Recruitment Processes

The other important process in any organisation is the strategic leadership process that involves recruiting the right and talented strategic management team. This process usually consists of the Chairperson, CEO, board of directors, non-executive directors, executive directors, and strategic senior management teams.

The process goal here is to have a competent strategic leadership with relevant skills, commercial experience, business ethics, and character qualities for creating and executing strategic objectives outlined in their master corporate strategy.

This extends to defining the culture of a business institution. Let us examine the term *culture*. What exactly does culture mean, simply asked? According to *thebalancecareers.com*, culture is the accumulation of employee personalities within an institution and how they behave and interact with each other.

The mission statement of the company may outline a specific code of ethics, clearly elaborating how the employees are expected to behave. However, an individual or a group of employees may resist and contradict that mission statement. An extremely important objective for the strategic leadership team is to make everyone feel safe by way of fair and equal treatment – from the most junior member of the company, all the way to the highest positions of management.

Culture is linked to leadership which is primarily defined and measured by the capability of the strategic leadership team to respond to employees who breach their values because their response communicates accepted behaviour without consequences or unaccepted behaviour with consequences.

In contrast also, how employees who exceed performance by aligning to the company values are rewarded and recognised for promotion is another leadership quality to be considered. (*Source: Harvard Business Review – hbr.org, Businessculture.org and Forbes.com*).

The focus of the board must be on recruiting the strategic leadership team (SLT) to direct the company with a work scope related to the strategic implication in the short, medium, and long-term perspectives. This role is critical because, without the right leadership team, any company can decline and even cease to exist. Examples of companies that had extensive leadership issues are Blockbuster, Kodak, Enron, Lehman Brothers, Arthur Anderson… and the list goes on and on.

Information Technology (IT) and Business Change Processes

The IT department exists to execute the corporate strategy by providing technology to improve customer satisfaction, protecting the organisation's technology assets including systems, data and servers, and implementing regulatory and compliance requirements. The key functions in the department are IT service desk and technical support, project management office (PMO), project delivery, information security, systems infrastructure, information systems, IT operations, IT administration, and communications. These are the expected functions in the IT department, but each organisation will always have its unique structure.

This department is crucial to an HPO because the organisation requires efficient IT processes and innovative technology in each function to help design a robust business operating model that has the sustainability to implement the corporate strategy. Without efficient IT processes, corporate strategy cannot be executed to the required standard. That's the reason why process definition and implementation within an organisation are vital in achieving the overall strategy.

The business change department ensures that the change strategy linked to the corporate strategy is effectively implemented through the processes performed by the IT department, and other shared-services departments, and is based on the business operating model in an organised and structured method. The goal is to minimise disruption by focusing on enhancing customers' experience, and product quality, ensuring the emotional transformation of employees by adapting to the change required, and effecting productivity optimisation for internal as well as external stakeholders.

Change management capability is aimed at instituting the best practices, adherence to governance frameworks, systems, processes, procedures, policies, and engaging people with the right skills to execute the strategy. The goal is to build an organisation that can deliver change by way of competent employees, competitive operational capabilities, integrated processes, and a dynamic structure.

If a critical business change is not implemented efficiently, the project or programme failure could have a significant impact on costs and the financial position of the organisation. These costs are typically associated with project delays and reputation damage, both internally and externally, that impact customers and critical stakeholders. The cost implication may affect the brand equity, resulting in revenue depreciation, customer loss, market-share reduction, and negative values reflected on the financial statements.

The IT department oversees their shared-service processes and operating model processes which must be driven by the corporate strategy. The strategic leadership teams must be aligned in providing the required IT funding to achieve the change.

Programme Management Office Processes (PMOs)

The fundamental goal of PMOs is to execute the organisation's corporate strategy by setting the required pre-investment project appraisal processes, requesting funding, and performing project delivery processes for best practices. The function is additionally responsible for monitoring expenditures based on variance analysis of actual spending against budgets. This function specifically aims to ensure that projects being delivered are providing a positive rate of return and shareholders' wealth is invested in value-adding projects. In most companies, the PMO function is embedded as a part of the IT department. According to consultancy firm Gartner, it is predicted that the PMO function is likely to decline because of the digital revolution and integrated with change management functions. (*Source: CIO.com*).

The key drivers for PMO efficiency in outlining the costs to deliver projects are based on multiple factors and below are some examples:

- PMO competence and skill sets.
- PMO knowledge and understanding of corporate strategy objectives.
- Business stakeholder support and collaboration.

- Project delivery processes and frameworks being selected with the most widely used methodologies being Agile, Scrum, Agile/Scrum, Kanban, Scrumban, Waterfall, Agile/Waterfall, Six-Sigma, Project Management Professional. Prince2, and Project Integrating Sustainable Methods.
- Project resource requirements and team size from project managers, business analysts, developers, data engineers, business SMEs, business sponsors, third-party suppliers, testing and quality assurance (QA), release teams and business readiness teams.
- Project resource competence and skillsets.
- Project delivery templates and documentation depending on the size of the project, being small, medium or large. If a small project requires sixty pages for a business case to request funding, there is an exceptional efficiency issue. The project templates must be lean, focusing on information that adds value to customer satisfaction, with the main goal of assisting the funding committee to provide approval or reject projects.
- Time frames to realistically execute projects based on project methodology and determining the phases of projects.
- Organisation bureaucracy in making project decisions quickly.
- How complex the business operating model is in relation to executing business transformation or business change.
- Financial analysis processes based on the availability of data analytics to create reports while tracking and monitoring project performance.

PMO efficiency is critical to selecting and executing projects that generate company positive returns because the figures significantly impact the valuation of earnings before interest and tax (EBITDA) on financial statements.

Business Operating Model Processes

In most companies, each department or business unit and function has specific business processes that contribute directly or indirectly to creating and delivering products and services to their customers. These processes make up their business operating model and business architecture.

The business operating model is comprised of people, technology, systems, processes, procedures, governance, business policies, data analytics, and business performance measurement reporting.

Process maps are critical for any business operating model because the roles and responsibilities define the workload that is performed in each function.

The process of organisational design, in turn, helps formulate resource requirements and resource optimisation to create the company's business structure and three-tier business organisational chart. The more automated and more value-adding activities are performed, the less manual human resources will be required. This scenario will result in reduced HR costs for salaries and promoting sustainable operations, with better services being provided to customers, thus increasing customer satisfaction.

Risk Management Processes

Process definition plays a significant role in identifying and managing any organisation-wide risk. Risk management can be performed by identifying risks in the processes and introducing specific controls to mitigate those risks.

The risk process framework effectively establishes a way of managing categorised risks based on the prioritisation of strategy, business operations, and shared functions.

Chapter three provides more context relating to how processes contribute to robust risk management governance when it comes to business risks, non-business risks, financial risks and overall corporate risk for that orgnisation.

Business Performance Measurement Processes

To ensure that the business is progressing in the right direction to achieve its strategy, the leadership team needs to define the key critical success factors (CSFs) for measuring and monitoring performance. This measurement and assessment can be performed on a daily, weekly, or monthly basis to enable decisions to be made.

The key benefits of monitoring CSFs include a traditional approach employed as a balanced scorecard. (Dr Robert Kaplan and David Norton, 1992). The main objective of a balanced score is to measure business performance by linking the business strategy with the key performance indicators (KPIs) for determining if the targets are being achieved or not being achieved.

The scorecard consists of four perspectives – namely: financial perspective, customer perspective, internal process, and lastly, learning growth. This is effectively a basic concept, and every institution can introduce their specific business performance measurements to suit the required CSFs and benchmark the actual results against the projected forecasts.

Strategic Critical Success Factors for any Organisation

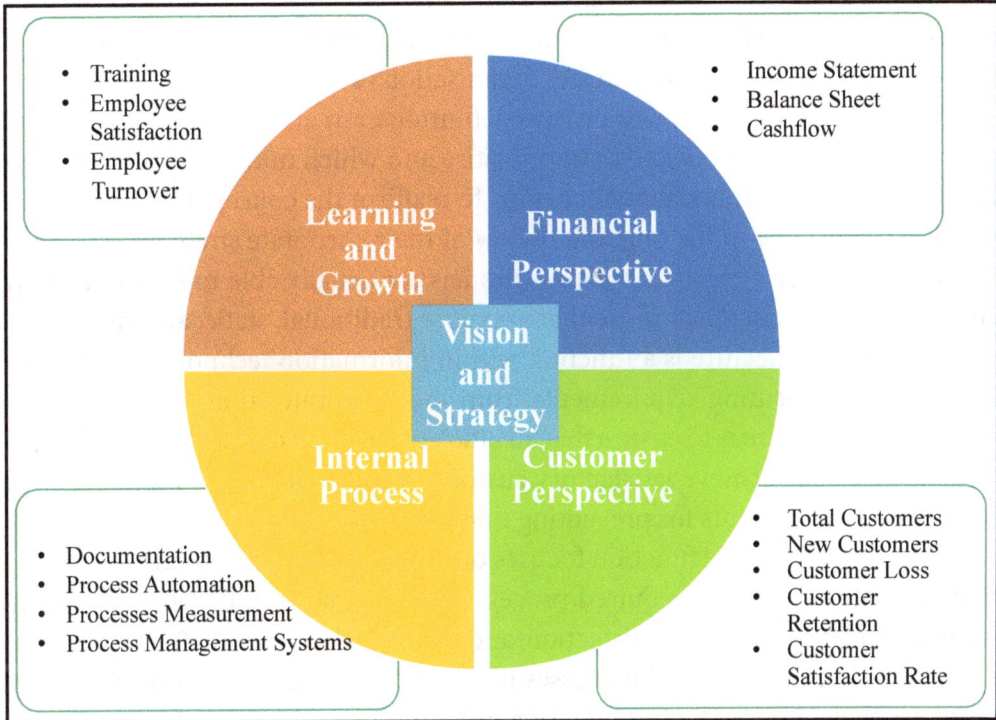

Figure 2: *Balanced Score Card (Source: Supplychaintoday.com)*

The scorecard can be construed as the strategic dashboard of a company with a consolidated perspective using data analytics to present data visualisations.

The availability of information is dependent on business intelligence, reporting on processes and software, and the data analytics system infrastructure to display business measurements easily and accurately.

Linking Business Architecture to Corporate Strategy, Strategic Leadership Recruitment, IT, PMO, CSFs Performance Measurement, and Business Operating Model Processes

The emphasis here is that corporate strategy, strategic leadership recruitment processes, IT, PMO, CSF performance measurement, and business operating model processes, together contribute to any organisation's success.

Also, without integration or process definitions, any company can quickly lose direction about which objectives to prioritise and which not, particularly during exceptional events. This statement begins to reaffirm the concept that companies which are proactive in the ongoing review of their corporate strategies and have fewer bureaucracies on their business models are usually able to introduce new changes more quickly than those that are more traditional, static, and rigid.

Business architecture is a function within information technology that is responsible for executing requirements from the corporate strategy. The role for business architecture is to ensure that an efficient business operating model infrastructure exists to achieve satisfactory customer experience and compliance with regulatory requirements for preventing fines and breaches.

The business change function focuses on understanding the company's direction and introducing the required process transformation in the short and long term to achieve customer satisfaction and loyalty. The year, 2020 saw a global economic crisis with many businesses having to experiencing significant continuity problems due to the COVID-19 pandemic. There are many factors at play, but the top-most reasons that resulted in companies facing going concern issues are mostly linked to the factor of not quickly changing their corporate strategies, overhauling the IT, PMO, and operating model processes, and business architecture for delivering products and services in the new and emerging digital shopping channels, cutting across customer segments.

That said, process management has been demonstrated and existed even before the times of Henry Ford in 1914. The automobile company developed assembly lines in their factories driven by business process techniques to achieve operational efficiencies and KPIs. The process management methodology continues to evolve today, involving artificial intelligence (AI) and robotics and contributing to organisations' success, profitability, and customer satisfaction. (*Ford.com*)

Chapter One

Operational Excellence Strategy and Process Architecture Set-Up

---

Chapter Introduction

THIS CHAPTER UNDERSCORES that for successful process management implementation and sustainability within an organisation, funding, sponsorship, and positive support from the board and senior management are required for a further desirable cascading effect on the operations.

The operational excellence strategy affects cross functions that need investment at every stage, right from setting up the process architecture to introducing and establishing an effective excellence culture, supported top-down or bottom-up.

As the process architecture set-up and sustainability impact the strategic, tactical, and operational levels, a planned extensive collaboration and support in the form of cultural transformation from all employees across the enterprise is required.

Chapter Learning Outcomes

In this chapter, your key learning objectives will include:

- The importance of operational excellence strategy for process design.
- Setting up a robust process architecture framework and infrastructure.
- Company-wide process levels and hierarchies across business functions.
- Culture transformation to support continuous learning at company-wide level.
- Process benefits and integration with artificial intelligence (AI).

Overall, this chapter sets the pre-requisites or foundation for a successful process management architecture and process culture to support business change.

Operational Excellence Strategy

This is a decision made in an organisation at the corporate strategy or executive level to design processes for that company. The main goal of process design is to achieve cost reduction through minimising inefficiencies and non-value-adding activities and, at the same time, contributing to improving performance, customer experience, product quality design profitability, and market share.

Investing in process transformation requires funding from the board, infusion of skilled process resources, process software installation and training, and collaboration with multiple stakeholders to document the processes using the industry-standard software. This activity needs senior leadership sponsorship to be carried out and sustained at a company-wide level, from strategy to operations.

The performance measurements of each process determine the workload currently executed, therefore contributing to framing the future organisational structure and the number of employees required in each department and function. A part of this 'towards excellence' activity involves adding new processes to keep in tune with time and discontinuing those that are no longer adding value to the overall corporate strategy and competitiveness in the business landscape.

The process performance metrics can also be effectively used to understand the root cause of problems impacting cross functions. Significantly, these bring to the fore the urgent need for introducing the correct solutions such as automation, simplifying workflows, replacing legacy systems with advanced industry-leading technology, merging functional processes, removing duplication, providing training, and recruiting the right resources with the required skill sets.

Examples of Company-wide Processes for Organisations

Company-wide Processes (*Source: Mckinsey.com and PWC.com*)

Corporate Strategy Processes

- Business strategy
- Relationship management
- Mergers and acquisition
- Other strategy processes

Core Business Processes

- Business operations from the front, middle to back-office functions

Shared Services Processes

- Finances
- Human resources (HR)
- Health and safety
- Information technology and systems
- Digital technology
- Product design, research, and development
- Sales and marketing
- Procurement and purchase-to-pay
- Financial auditing
- Financial and investment advisory
- Risk, compliance, and legal services
- Facility services

- Environmental expertise
- Corporate social responsibility and sustainability

Centre of Excellence Teams for Process Management

The functions responsible for process management in most organisations are usually the centre of excellence or business change or business transformation, and/ or IT departments. However, the functions vary depending on the organisation.

In collaboration with the HR department, the aforementioned functions will work in a concerted way on strategic communication, cultural transformation, process artefacts, and enable implementation targets.

Business Process Hierarchy and Levels

I would highly recommend kick-starting process analysis by creating the business process hierarchy levels and then identifying the processes performed in each function. If this information is readily available, process analysis will be simplified.

Business process hierarchy is a valuable tool used to outline the processes performed in an organisation based on respective functions. The information is critical not only to the organisational structure design but also for defining the value-adding activities required and linking them to the overall corporate strategy.

The business process hierarchy contributes to shaping the future business operations, including functional activities like investment or discontinuation. Investment can range from technology, people, processes, and data reporting analytics. While choosing the right hierarchy, it's critical to link the organisation's design and service lines allocated alongside each function.

Business process hierarchies are the strategic scopes of a company, and this information must be addressed at the strategic directorial level who would define the scope of current and future operating models including the end-to-end business.

Business Process Hierarchy and Levels

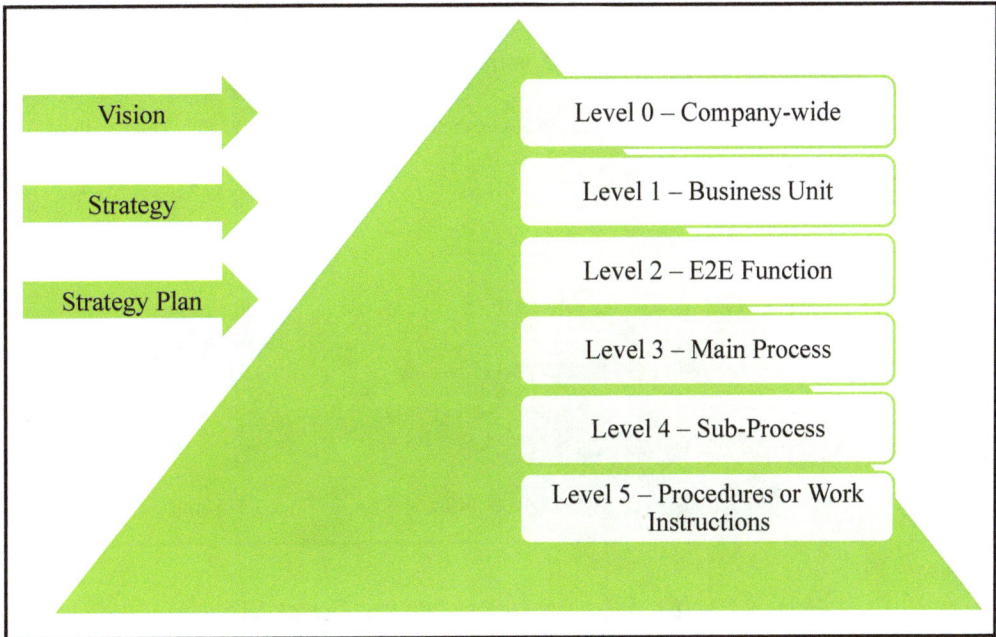

Figure 3: *Business Process Levels (Source: SAP.com)*

The business process hierarchy and the constituent levels together form a great framework for commencing structural build-up and also for breaking down the processes within an organisation. Otherwise, the process activity would be more complicated to perform without a framework or reference guide.

The bedrock of this principle is a simple list of all the processes performed in each function and structure as shown in Figure 4. Below are the examples of each level:

- Level 0 – Company-wide: Amazon Online Stores
- Level 1 – Business Unit: Business Operations UK
- Level 2 – E2E Function: Customer Service
- Level 3 – Main Process: Complaints
- Level 4 – Sub-Process: Phone Complaints
- Level 5 – Procedures/ Work Instructions: Phone Complaints

Simplified Company-wide Business Process Catalogue

L0	Company-wide		
L1	1. Corporate Strategy	2. Business Operations	3. Shared Service Functions
L2	1.1 Business Strategy	2.1 Front Office	3.1 Human Resources (HR)
	1.2 Relationship Management	2.2 Middle Office	3.2 Information Technology
	1.3 Add L2 Processes	2.3 Back Office	3.3 Add L2 Processes
L3	Add L3 Main Processes	Add L3 Main Processes	Add L3 Main Processes
L4	Add L4 Sub Processes	Add L4 Sub Processes	Add L4 Sub Processes
L5	Add L5 Work Instructions	Add L5 Work Instructions	Add L5 Work Instructions

Figure 4: *Level 0 to 5 Business Process Catalogue (Source: SAP.com)*

The volume of the business processes will vary depending on the activities performed in each function and how the organisational structure has been designed.

The goal here is to provide a holistic picture of how the business processes are structured from Level 0 to Level 5 to have an end-to-end view.

From Figure 4, it's evident there would be drill-down functionality enabling a more vivid view of the main and sub-processes if a process mapping software is used. This is the reason why this mapping software is recommended for process management, and it's obvious that without it, the drill-down capability would be more complicated to exact processes at the different levels.

Process mapping software like ARIS, IBM, Nimbus, and many other industry leading process tools have great features and functionality to structure the process levels and users can filter to view the levels based on the information required.

Industries by Process Complexity

Highest Process Complexity (Heavy Industries)	Moderate Process Complexity (Light Industries)
Aerospace	Financial Services
Transport	Logistics
Computer	Agriculture
Telecommunication	Education
Automobile	Pharmaceutical
Marine	Food
Defence	Health Care
Manufacturing	Hospitality
Construction	Entertainment
Pharmaceutical	Specific Downstream Energy
Energy	Information Technology
Mining	News Media
Electronics	Music
Robotics	Worldwide Web
	Advertising
	Creative
	Fashion
	Publishing
	Retail

Figure 5: *Process Complexity by Industry (Source: Mckinsey.com and Statista.com)*

Some processes are too complex or hazardous and simply cannot be performed by human resources. In such situations, humans are specifically replaced by automation and robotic resources to prevent the occurrence of adverse situations.

Business Process Management Software

"Business Process Management Software (BPMS) is a software for capturing, documenting, mapping, creating workflows, recording, storing, analysing, measuring, improving, and automating business processes. The essence is to have all company-wide business processes in a centralised location to assist with SWOT analysis for that organisation." (*Source: PWC.com*)

Choosing the right business process software is critical to achieving these goals. The software must contain advanced technological features for linking with the corporate strategy. Most importantly, the software must be able to integrate with the existing systems in the organisational operating model for architecture maximisation.

BPM software can be used effectively to achieve the following benefits:

- Listing all processes that exist at the company-wide level and performed by each function.
- Assigning roles and responsibilities to the business functions responsible for maintaining and updating the processes as they evolve. This is to ensure business process ownership within the business enterprise.
- Automating processes using workflows and linking with the front, middle, and back-end systems to improve the process cycle times.
- Clarifying which business processes are value-adding and which ones are not, and therefore should not be performed.
- Identifying gaps in the corporate strategy to ensure that the right business functions receive the level of investment required to improve operational performance and customer satisfaction.
- Contributing to corporate planning where accurate data and business process information have been provided to the strategy teams.
- Providing input to the business design and HR requirements for the current and future business models based on corporate strategy.
- Business units such as the centre of excellence and business change receive investment for ensuring that BPM is managed for continuous improvement.
- Performing root cause analysis, accurate problem identification, and problem-solving information as it pertains to the business process to prevent problems from reoccurring.
- Providing solutions for customer experience and customer journeys, including supply chain efficiency.

- Ensuring standardisation and adherence to company policies.
- Contributing to making sure that the business is measuring the correct metrics to assess company performance and strategic planning.

Overall, BPS is linked to business architecture as a key component contributing to data compilation and data analytics for accurately measuring a company's performance.

Types of Business Process Maps and Templates

There are many types of business process maps, however, this book will focus on the following three types of flowcharts and process maps:

- Cross-functional Process Maps with BPMN Symbols
- Cross-functional Process Maps without BPMN Symbols
- Non-Cross-functional Process Maps without BPMN Symbols

Cross-Functional Process Maps with Swim Lanes and BPMN

Business process modelling notation (BPMN) provides industry-standard diagram symbols used for mapping and documenting business processes. There is a logic to how the diagrams correctly depict the business process flow.

The BPMN symbols are available in most business process mapping tools. The industry software business process tools include Visio, Aris, Nimbus, Camunda, Mega and many other recognisable solutions. One of the major benefits of BPMN is the ability to achieve consistency related to best practices. The process software has the functionality to select the pre-defined BPMN template and analysts can have the flexibility to choose other symbols on the templates. BPMN templates can be defaulted where required to ensure that mapping processes achieve business consistency and process design standardisation on their presentations.

Imagine if multiple business process maps were documented, each with different methodologies, frameworks, and designs. Process mapping would be confusing to the business stakeholders then. Presenting the information on a standard template in a simple manner is thus the only way to ensure consistency, accuracy, and true understanding for all stakeholders reading the process information.

Example of BPMN Symbols and Meaning

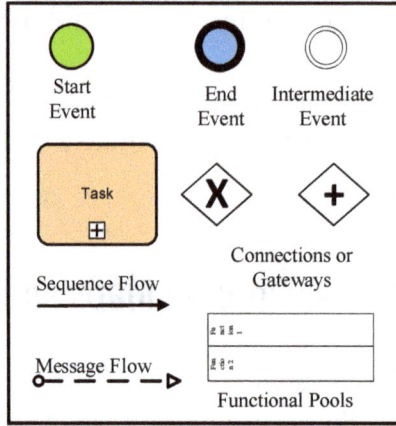

Figure 6: *Symbols for BPMN Diagrams (Source: BPMN.org)*

Horizontal Cross-functional Process Map with BPMN Symbols

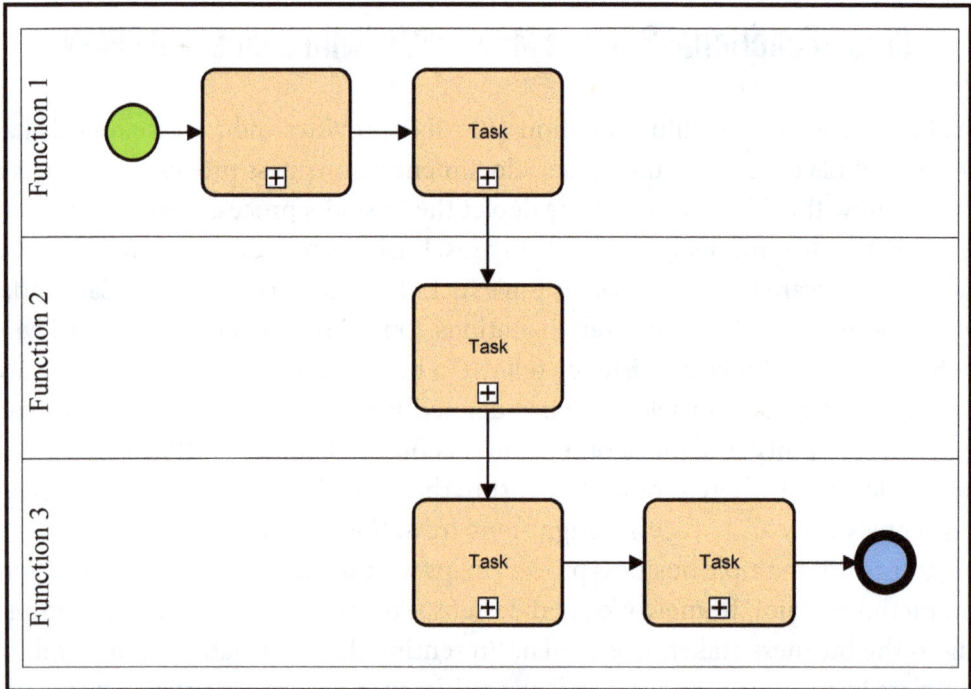

Figure 7: *BPMN Symbols with Swim-Lane (Source: BPMN.org)*

Vertical Cross-functional Process Map with BPMN Symbols

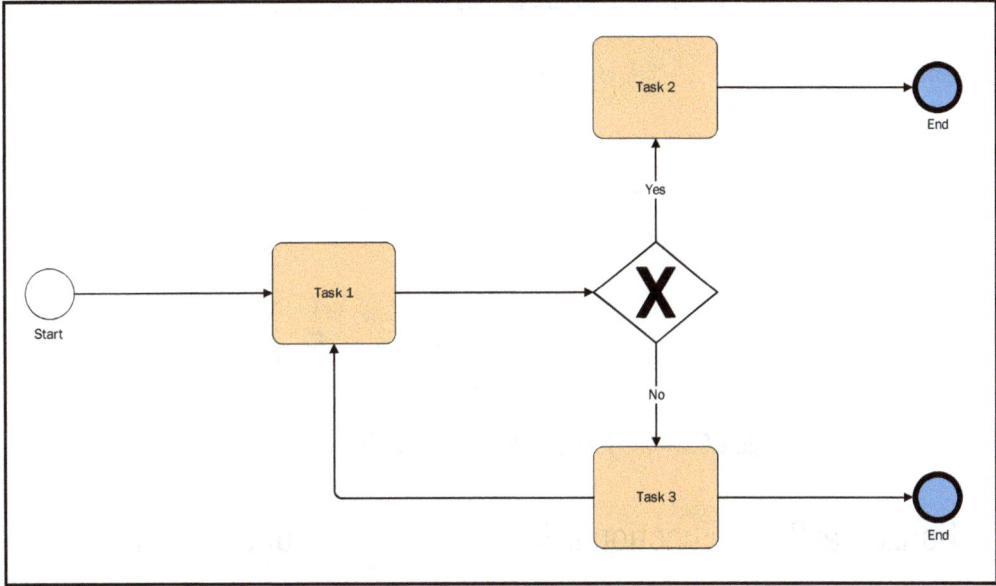

Figure 8: *BPMN Symbols with No Swim-lane (Source: BPMN.org)*

Cross-Functional Process Maps without BPMN Symbols

There are scenarios where processes can be documented using the generic symbols without BPMN using Visio and other software.

Visio is a user-friendly software that can be used for documenting cross-functional process maps without integrating the BPMN symbols.

These symbols are all industry best practices and accepted in global business change specifically concerning process mapping.

Example of Symbols without BPMN

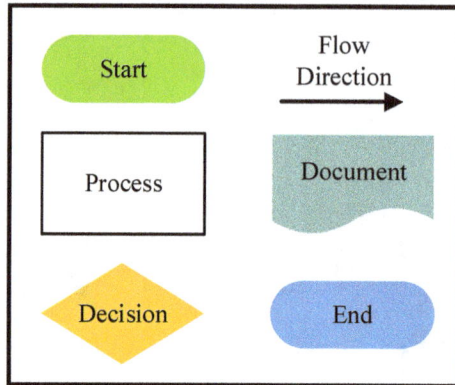

Figure 9: *Symbols without BPMN (Source: Microsoft.com)*

Horizontal Cross-Functional Process Map without BPMN Symbols

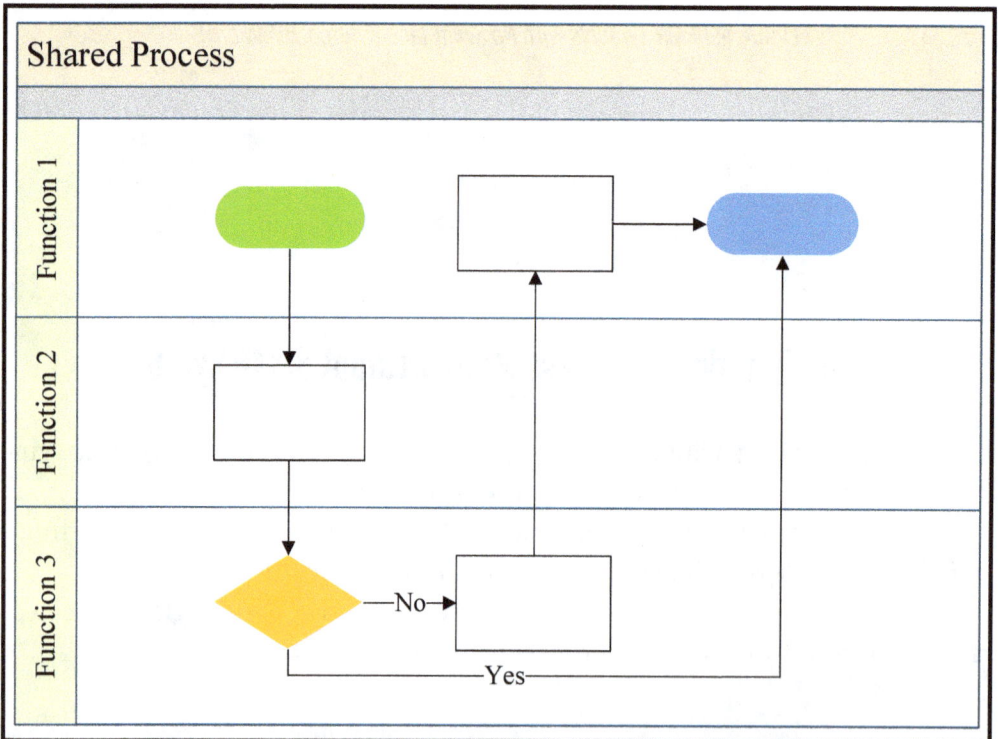

Figure 10: *Horizontal Swim-Lane but without BPMN (Source: Microsoft.com)*

Vertical Cross-Functional Process Map without BPMN Symbols

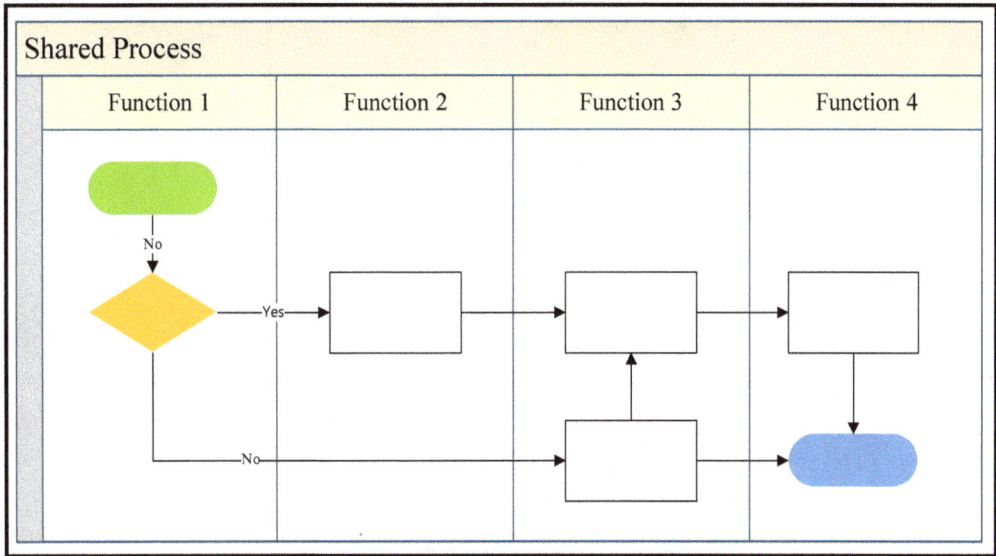

Figure 11: *Vertical Swim-Lane but without BPMN (Source: Microsoft.com)*

Non-Cross-Functional Process Maps without BPMN Symbols

This is a basic process map that uses generic business process symbols without BPMN standards. Some of the symbols are similar to BPMN diagrams, but there are also many differences and objectives for selecting this type of process map.

These diagrams are available in most business process mapping tools with industry-standard software. The symbols selected vary based on the business process map being documented, and the basic diagrams for illustration purposes are as follows:

Example of Symbols without BPMN

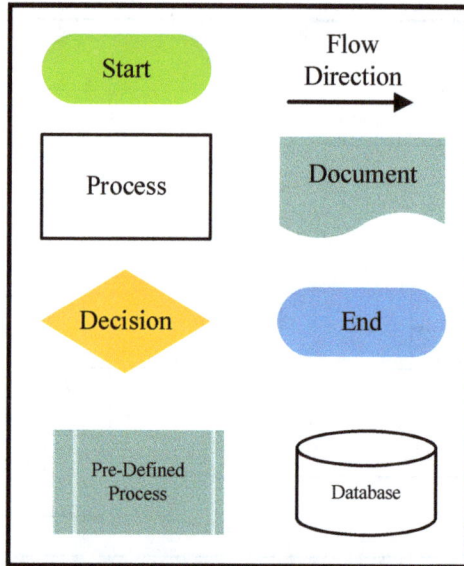

Figure 12: *Diagram Symbols without BPMN (Source: Microsoft.com)*

Example of Process Map without Swim-Lanes or BPMN

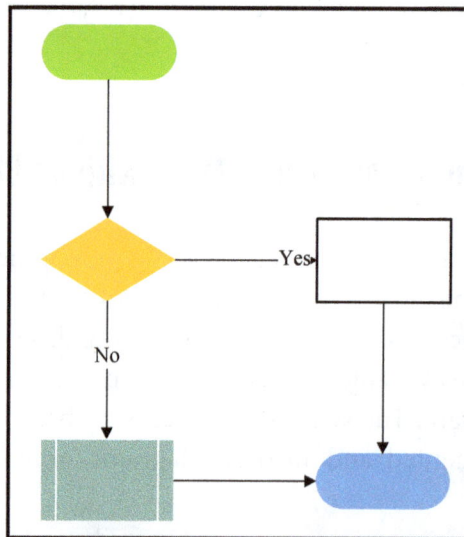

Figure 13: *Process Map without Swim-Lane or BPMN (Source: Microsoft.com)*

Business Culture Transformation for Process Excellence

Creating business culture transformation for process excellence starts with the support and sponsorship of the executive and senior management teams.

Once the leadership has provided process approval, strategic communication will be required to be sent across the whole organisation explaining the new ways of working (the framework that have been chosen, for example, Six Sigma and other leading industry process frameworks), earmarking along with this the roles and responsibilities of the employees in supporting process excellence.

There must be several communications that are required to be sent to business stakeholders, starting with the whole organisation, cascading further down to specific functions and process owners or heads of departments. Allocating process ownership is a great initiative for engagement, collaboration, ownership, and continuous improvement across the organisation. Setting and deciding process artefacts as part of a standard requirements for any business change is one of the ways of establishing the process culture. Then, continuously promoting process benefits through workshops and introducing the new frameworks to be used across operations in day-to-day activities (or when making project changes across all operational teams) is of vital importance for sustaining a process culture.

Sharing information and metrics about how processes have improved business operations, including cost savings, customer experience, and profitability, is yet another method of getting support from the operational teams.

There must be a dedicated function responsible for process excellence that is well-supported and recognised across the organisation for long-term success.

Business Process Management and Reporting Capability

Business process measurements vary by business size. The common ones are cycle time, cost, resource productivity, waste and reworks, compliance, frequency, supplier value-chain effectiveness, and many other elements.

The metrics are the key performance indicators (KPIs) that measure how well the business is achieving its targets against the "actuals" or relative to historical performance for trend analysis in performance improvement.

Process measurements ensure that the root cause of the issue is addressed, the KPIs are used for performance monitoring after the change has have been implemented. The KPI assessment determine if the changes introduced have actually addressed the root cause or if the symptoms have been masked merely in a cosmetic way.

Some examples of process metrics for a Contact Centre which have been carefully selected include the following (*Source: Oracle.com*):

Process Metrics to Measure Resource Productivity

- Abandoned Calls: This metric is intricately linked to productivity and, most importantly, determines if a company has enough resources to answer customer calls or if too many unnecessary calls are being received in the contact centre due to inefficiencies of the operating model.
- Average Handling Time: This KPI is vital for measuring the overall productivity across call centre operations, both when agents answer the call and when the call has been completed with the customer. There must also be a trend analysis to determine if the specific agents usually take longer than the average time or if most agents take similar time frames to resolve issues depending on the category and complexity of the issue.

Process Metrics to Measure Cycle Time

- Average Time in the Queue: If agents are taking too long to answer customer calls, either they need more training to address customers for digital support or learn to resolve queries more quickly. Again, in the context of productivity, it is important to understand the reasons customers are calling. This is to ensure that this information is provided to them digitally or possibly connected to business operational issues.

Process Metrics to Measure Waste and Reworks

- Customer Complaints or Customer Dissatisfaction: These metrics specifically address the issue of quality and first-time resolution not achieved as expected by a customer. If a customer complains about the service or product, the issue usually involves process defects with the overall output in the organisation failing to satisfy their needs.

How Artificial Intelligence Adds Value to Process Mapping

BPM has many benefits in creating efficiencies to improve organisational performance. However, combining artificial intelligence (AI), robotics automation, and machine learning to the BPM model can generate further cost advantages, which include the following: (*Source: CMSWire.com*)

- Robotic process automation (RPA) is software driven by machine learning meant for replacing manual tasks and procedures with automated workflows on the business processes. The software can replace complex manual processes with sophisticated automated workflows, thereby increasing operational efficiency.
- Workflow optimisation to avoid the time spent on unnecessary tasks that do not add value to the organisation. Data analytics and artificial intelligence can provide information about how much time is spent on specific processes and suggest possible improvements.
- Predictive analysis can be used from machine learning automation to monitor datasets from the business processes, followed by prediction of future trends, customer behaviour, and preferences. Access to this valuable information can enable businesses to make important decisions more quickly, reduce costs, increase revenue streams and explore new opportunities for high business performance.
- The said information can be used to achieve a better customer experience through AI analytics that predicts customer behaviour and provides insights. Although intricately linked to predictive analytics benefits, the focus is on customer experience innovation, operational excellence, process improvement, and competitive optimisation.
- Competitive advancement through efficiency, accuracy, speed, superior product design, better customer service, and greater customer satisfaction.
- Better decision-making capabilities through machine learning algorithms resulting in a clearer understanding of data and business problems, leading to judicious recommendations for the next best action. Furthermore, the staff receive adequate encouragement to come up with innovative solutions that would never have been explored without AI analytics and technological advancements.

How Business Process Mapping Adds Financial Value

Business processes are essential to companies for several reasons, but most importantly, to achieve their corporate strategies. The targets could be for company expansion, downsizing, or continuous improvement. (*Source: PWC.com*)

We will look closely into some of the common reasons behind companies investing in business process mapping on their value chain:

- Companies can respond rapidly to urgent business changes such as COVID-19 or to opportunities associated with planned business transformation or new opportunities.
- Businesses can improve customer journeys, customer experience, and customer satisfaction through process transformation of product design and customer service, which increases revenue and market share.
- The organisations must be compliant with industry regulations. The business processes make sure that companies implement the regulatory requirements faster, thus preventing avoidable delays in this regard. Integrating compliance becomes a life cycle, which means that business processes are more understandable to the employees.
- Companies frequently need changes when new regulations are set, which in turn sets the demand for new ways of working.
- Improve employee productivity through automation of repetitive elements in regular specified workflows, thus eliminating waste and reducing costs for non-value-adding activities within the organisation.
- Process mapping can facilitate streamlining of functions that help the company to become flexible and agile in times of change. Furthermore, it paves the way for customising the requirements and new organisational design for transforming business operations.
- Bring clarity to the operating model to ensure standardisation and consistency between various departments, business units, and functions within all levels of the organisation.
- Besides, business processes help reduce risks and promote a value-adding culture. The visibility of these processes leads to efficiencies and concentration since they give the organisation a chance to outline and determine the processes which are more value-adding than others. This approach results in savings of resources or headcount and enables the taking of prudent investment decisions for business change. The company also becomes

more competitive which increases its chances of capturing a greater market share.

- The processes have also played an indispensable role in designing, executing, and monitoring metrics that help reduce risks at all levels of the organisation. Transparency and compliance are the other benefits gained.

- Training of employees through documentation of processes and procedures (training manuals or work instructions) to ensure consistency and standardisation in services being provided is yet another worthwhile undertaking. The goal is to ensure that quality services are provided to customers to secure their trust and satisfaction.

- Appropriate solutions are implemented to improve the business operations because an accurate understanding of the activities is captured. Overall, it leads to increased performance, profitability, and competitor sustainability.

- Process mapping promotes ownership, accountability, and continuous improvement initiatives by deploying the Responsible, Accountable Consult and Inform (RACI) framework, which defines who is responsible and needs to be consulted when performing that process.

- Mapping increases the knowledge and understanding of the institution, from strategy to operations, providing clear visibility of all business processes within each department and how resources can be accurately allocated for achieving the business strategy. Better and informed decisions are made, which leads to improvement of business performance.

Business Process Benchmarking with Competitors

Fast Food Chain Restaurants Process Benchmarking

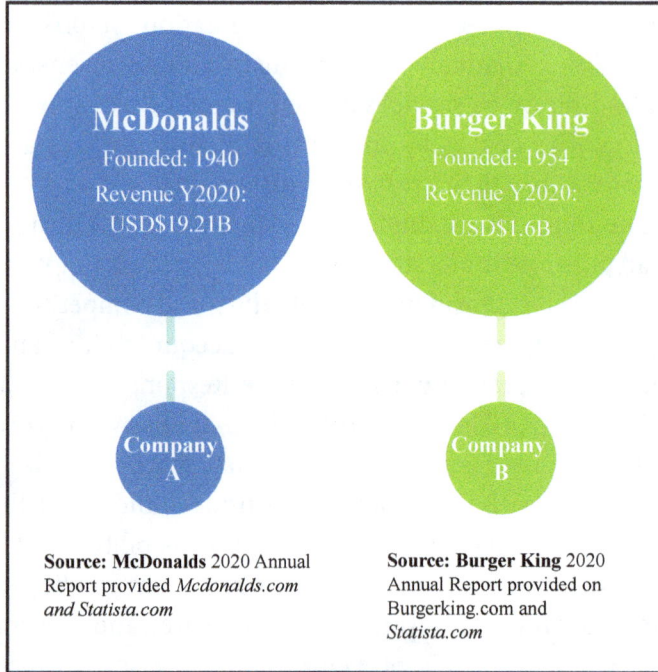

Figure 14: *Fast Food Chain Benchmarking with Competitors*

In this section, McDonald's and Burger King, the two largest fast-food chain restaurants in the world, are being benchmarked for revenue, franchises, global restaurants, and advertising expenditure. The main goal from a process perspective is to see how both the companies performed by considering the robustness of their processes which determine customer experience and customer satisfaction. An increase, year after year, in the four metrics in such saturated competitive markets with similar services and the new generation of healthy diets show how robust the processes of McDonald's are when it comes to marketing strategies and operational efficiencies to attract global customers since its foundation in 1940.

McDonald's

Worldwide Revenue: 19.21B (USD) 2020
Franchise and Property Revenue: 10.73B (USD) 2020
Number of Restaurants Worldwide: 39,198
Advertising Expenditure: 654.7M (USD), 2020
Source: *Statista.com*

Burger King

Worldwide Revenue: 1.6 B (USD) 2020 and 1.78B (USD) 2019
Franchise and Property Revenue: 1.54 B (USD)
Number of Restaurants Worldwide: 18,625
Advertising Expenditure: 287M (USD)
Source: *Statista.com*

How Business Processes Contribute to Business Continuity

In setting up the process architecture and process framework, the operational excellence strategy linked to corporate strategy will determine the resources required for process management in sustaining business continuity processes. Process management contributes to the day-to-day running of the business; therefore, when exceptional scenarios such as COVID-19 occur, it's the business processes outlined in the business continuity plan that will enable the organisation to recover from disruption and continue to generate revenue.

Business Process Management Model

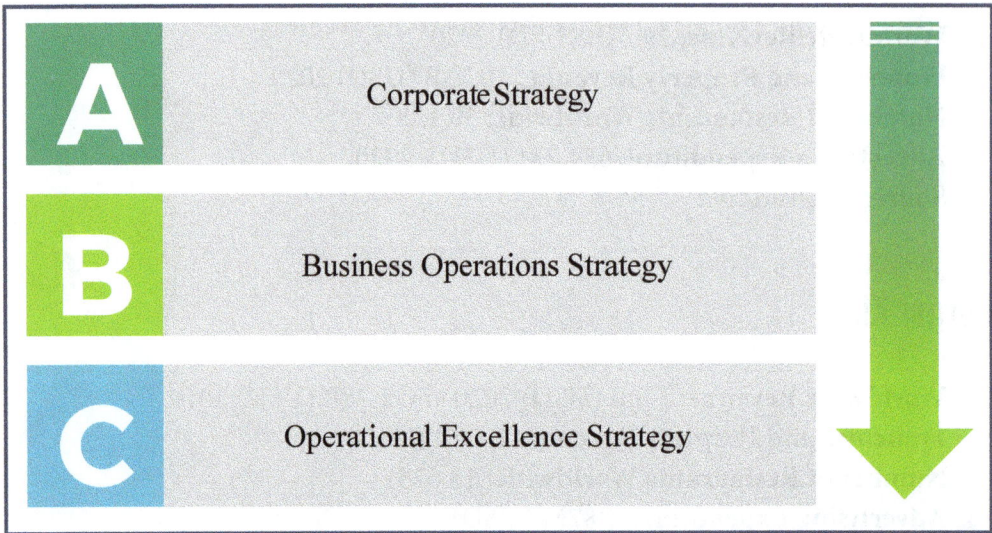

Figure 15: *Business Process Management and Operational Excellence*

As we experienced the pandemic in 2020, everything was shut down, with virtually all employees compelled to work from home. It's pertinent to mention that it was business processes documentation and technology that enabled some businesses to operate at maximum capacity and others at a significantly lower capacity.

The fundamental processes in the business continuity plan require all critical employees of a company to perform their respective roles and responsibilities. This framework makes sure that the company is operating the business as usual with customer experience unaffected in a negative way and profitability margins maintained for business continuity purposes in the long term.

The other key element of how processes contribute to business continuity is having a set of updated and well-documented business recovery procedures along with data backup to prevent loss of data and/or the absence of critical opportunities.

Case Example

Binder Dijker Otte (BDO), an international accounting and consulting firm, generated revenues of 10.3B USD in 2020. Their commitment to long-term investment has focused on process automation for operational efficiency. (*Source: BDO.com*)

According to the accounting firm, process automation is highly prioritised on the operational agendas of most British organisations.

The requirement to invest in process automation in most companies is being supported by senior leadership, such as Chief Financial Officers (CFOs) and Financial Directors (FDs).

Specific statistics and surveys to corroborate that there's a thrust on investment in process automation in 2019 are provided below:

- 87% of businesses introduced process improvement and automated critical business processes to improve their operating models.
- 21% of CFOs had prioritised process automation investment for the next five years to improve operational efficiency.
- 9% of most business operational expenditures was earmarked to be spent on data analytics, artificial intelligence, and process automation.

Process automation can only be achieved by setting up the right process architecture and having the right process tools for analysis, measurements, and solution design to replace manual procedures.

Having a robust process architecture and infrastructure is a prerequisite to arriving at the implementation stage of process automation as a solution.

From the statistics provided by BDO, which is one of the largest international accounting firms, they observed unmistakable evidence of the significance of process mapping and process automation.

Since COVID-19 in 2020, process mapping and automation have become top priorities for companies in ensuring that their businesses are operating at maximum capacity and increasing profit margins.

Summary

The closing lessons in this section underline that successful process implementation requires investment in the right process-skilled resources, usage of process software for process documentation, carefully selected process measurements, and a transformed culture across the whole organisation.

Support from senior management is critical to shifting the culture at operational levels and getting the support needed to optimise process efficiencies.

If the department or function performing process projects has not been set up strategically in getting visibility and the right skills to execute, the benefits of processes, unfortunately, will remain elusive.

The above examples used for benchmarking and the case study demonstrate how processes, as a methodology and performance measurement, provide a significant contribution to company revenue and net profitability.

Without careful identification and analysis of organisational processes, a business can be making wrong decisions that will have a negative impact on its future in the concerned sector particularly in the short or long term timescale.

Chapter Two

Defining Business Process Mapping

Chapter Introduction

HERE, THE MAIN GOAL is to demonstrate that high-level process information can be used as an input for corporate strategy analysis. Additionally, this information can also be useful for providing process frameworks and methodologies while creating both corporate strategy processes and detailed operational process maps to assist with project or programme change.

Chapter one has outlined the prerequisites in setting up process architecture for achieving process optimisation. This chapter addresses the misconception that process information and process mapping specifically add value when it comes to documenting detailed operational activities in business functions.

This book, therefore, provides a new lens for scrutinising the misstatement by showing that process information and process frameworks can add value for the executive teams to making quick and strategic decisions.

Chapter Learning Outcomes

The key learning topics in this chapter will cover the following:

- Definition of process maps.
- How process information adds value for quick strategic decision-making.

- How to design corporate strategy processes.
- How to design operational current state and future state processes.
- Examples of process maps documented using multiple software programs such as Visio, ARIS, Lucid Charts, and Nimbus.
- Robust process management for business continuity.
- Example of process benchmarking between global recognised brands.

This chapter effectively provides the structures and models that will be used to design and perform process analysis from strategy to operational activities.

Business Process Mapping Overview

There is extensive debate regarding business process mapping; however, with the scope of different business units in a business entity, how would you get the management to see business activities similarly?

In addition, how would you get the cross-operational teams within a company to achieve the same level of understanding about the strengths, weaknesses, opportunities, and risks at different enterprise levels of the organisation?

Here, we learn that business process maps are a solution planned to describe a company's activities using diagrams for visualisation purposes. Management and other stakeholders can have a similar vision and perform tasks in a similarly efficient way that contributes to executing the corporate strategy.

Before progressing to business process mapping, however, the first step must always be to create a process hierarchy or identify the list of processes that need to be reviewed in each function. This task is critical to establishing the process scope – the holistic process overview – prior to documenting the content, including the details that exist on a process map.

Oftentimes, those documenting processes start mapping the detailed business processes without having a big-picture view in understanding the corporate strategy and how the processes fit within the organisation at the functional level.

Taking this approach can be extremely limiting, ultimately restricting how an individual understands and creates effective business process solutions.

This book will discuss the progressive and innovative themes around business process mapping, including theory, techniques, standards, models, and benefits that contribute to delivering successful projects resulting in profitability and attainment of the high-performing organisation (HPO) status.

Defining Business Process Mapping

"Business process mapping (BPM) is a visual and diagrammatic technique describing the tasks in a particular sequence of activities from the start for getting something completed with the desired outcome. Effectively, it is the flow of data between departments, functions, and teams. The process map is used to define who is responsible for the activity by outlining the role, department, and function. (*Source: Microsoft.com*) "Processes can be structured and repeatable or unstructured and variable." (*Source: Gartner.com*)

BPM is carried out by defining the roles and responsibilities and documenting business process steps using advanced business process software tools, recommended symbols, standards, and principles.

Business process mapping is documented in several ways using multiple software and can be categorised between compliance regulatory business processes and non-compliance regulatory business processes.

Business processes that are compliance regulatory have specific requirements from the regulator, and non-adherence can lead to penalties, breaches, trading license revocation, and bad publicity in the mass media. Examples include the Sarbanes Oxley Act of 2002; FCA, FSA, and EU directives; and industry regulations.

Non-compliance regulatory business processes are supposed to be driven by the corporate strategy and are mostly targeted toward customer satisfaction, cost reduction, profitability, innovation, and market-share increments.

This leads to the pertinent question of where the business process mapping function fits within a company. The activity of documenting and maintaining business processes in most companies is performed by information technology (IT), business transformation, business change, and/or operational excellence. This decision is dependent on the organisational structure of that company.

There are many types of business process methodologies but the most widely used frameworks consist of the following techniques: business process mapping (BPM), Six Sigma, Lean Six Sigma, Lean, Agile, process mining, robotic process automation (RPA), Lean Kaizen, and value-stream mapping.

Business process mapping is not always simple and straightforward. It can be overly complex when optimising efficiency. This process is usually based on the system infrastructure's complications, the number of systems within the business process, lack of automated data availability, involvement of numerous steps in the process, multiple dependencies, and significant detailed documentation to capture the end-to-end process. The complicated business process will have a longer life cycle rather than a more efficient process with a shorter time frame to complete tasks and activities. (*Source: Appian.com*).

EXERCISE 1: Processes for Strategic Decision-Making

In this section, we will talk about how process information can be used as an input for strategic analysis, contributing to accurate and quick decisions being made. The best place to start is by following the process below:

- Identify the processes that exist in each function by listing them, and not performing any detailed analysis. This is like creating a process hierarchy as shown on page 16, Figure 4.
- Determine the number of processes that exist in each function.
- Which are the processes that are the most complex and carry the maximum risk at company-wide level or functional level?
- Which are the processes generating maximum revenue, customer interaction, and customer satisfaction for the business?
- Which are the processes that have the majority of problems and generate the bulk of the cost for maintenance at the operational level?
- Which processes generate maximum value and must be prioritised?

Process information must be easily available, otherwise, it can be easily gathered if no process definition exists in that organisation. The advantage of asking the process questions above, without having to perform detailed analysis, is to help the strategy teams understand what work is being performed at operational level and the cost to serve in maintaining the day-to-day activities.

The main objective for the process information is to ultimately understand how the processes identified in each function add value to the corporate strategy in increasing revenue, improving customer satisfaction, cutting costs, and improving operational efficiencies. The input, in effect, can contribute to deciding how resources and investments are allocated across the organisation.

EXERCISE 2: How to Design Corporate Strategy Processes

The goal here is to demonstrate that business process techniques are not only the tools key to documenting operational processes but are also valuable for designing corporate strategy processes, which have the utmost importance. One key requirement is to apply and extract principles from a variety of strategic models and create a future state-corporate strategy state.

Since corporate strategy is forward-looking, in this instance only, we are going to eliminate the need for extensive analysis of the current state. This activity is going to be very high-level, with the attention mostly on the future state.

As a background, we are aware that corporate strategy covers the main strategic plan of the whole organisation, which defines the overall values, purpose, mission, vision, objectives, and future direction of all business functions within a company.

The analysis in corporate strategy management will normally include product portfolio information, processes, resource optimisation, organisational design, governance, performance, and returns expected to derive value. (*Source: BCG.com*).

Value Creating Corporate Strategy Criteria

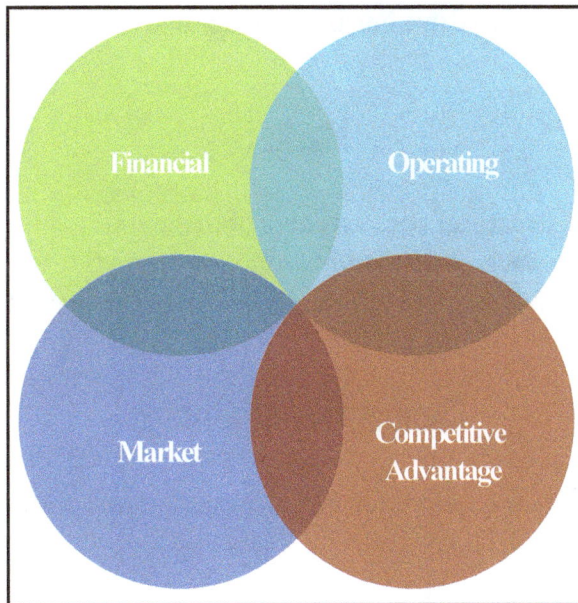

Figure 16: *Better Strategic Choices and Value Creation (Source: Mckinsey.com)*

The criteria of information that need to be included in the corporate strategy scope can be achieved by using the value creation corporate strategy choices model from *Mckinsey.com*. The model focuses on the following segments:

Financial

- Establish clear objectives for the business using accurate data analytics and insights to support strategic decisions.
- Maximise external factors and external risks in strategy creation.
- Optimise finances for value creation and where value is destroyed.
- Understand how to set up the critical success factors of the organisation.

Operating

- Formulate the right agile strategy processes to drive the business.
- Understand how to be effective at execution and updating of strategies.
- Take stakeholder needs into consideration.
- Educate managers on the transition to value-based thinking perspectives when making decisions.
- Understand how to drive business change and transformation.

Market

- Understand structural attractiveness of the market.
- Determine impacts of trends and economic disruptions such as COVID-19.
- Explore if there are opportunities in existing or new markets.

Competitive Advantage

- Define resources required for increasing economic profit and competition in those identified competitive markets.

The focus here is on the long-term view, how the strategic changes fit together across the organisation, and how the short-term and mid-term goals will support the corporate strategic objectives.

Rather than taking the long traditional approach, an agile methodology will be the sprint format needed to arrive more quickly at the provision of business values, objectives and company mission statements.

The corporate strategy is expected to be reviewed and revised continuously to ensure it is relevant and being achieved. Based on the BPR framework, the main agile phases would include the following stages outlined on the strategy process map:

Corporate Strategy Process

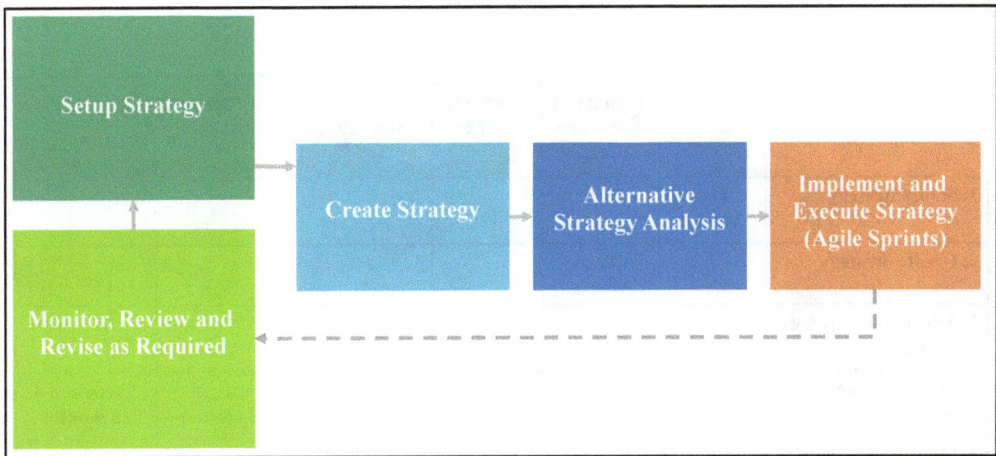

Figure 17: *Corporate Strategy Process Road Map*

Set-up Strategy Process

This phase will explain what the strategic project is trying to achieve, the strategic activities that need to be performed, high-level project plans, the resources required, stakeholder identification, communication collaboration, governance frameworks for best practices, reporting and tracking details, risk management, critical success evaluation, and cost-benefit analysis. In short, this information will be documented in a business case to highlight how value-based strategy can be accomplished and measured. The main outputs in this phase are the corporate strategy plan, corporate strategy resource on the project, and the corporate strategy process map.

Corporate Strategy Plan

A corporate strategy plan is important for showing the stages on the process, including the time allocated for completing each process phase. **The pace on the corporate strategy plan can either be slowed down or fast-tracked depending on the urgency to complete the life cycle.**

Corporate Strategy Plan

	January 2022	January to February 2022	February 2022	March to June 2022	July 2022 to July 2023	August 2023+
1. Setup Strategy	Two Weeks					
2. Create Strategy		Two Weeks				
3. Alternative Strategy Analysis			Two Weeks			
4. Implement and Execute Strategy				Execution < 3 months	Execution < 12 months	Execution > 12 months
5. Monitor, Evaluate and Amend				On-Going		
6. Revise as Needed				On-Going		

Figure 18: *Corporate Strategy High-level Plan*

The main goal is to have a big picture map that displays the work that will be performed, and the duration involved in completing the corporate strategy tasks.

Corporate Strategy Resource on the Project

The corporate strategy resource is the most fundamental because it defines both the corporate strategy process and the quality of the output expected. The expertise and skill set of the resource will help shape the quality of the final strategy.

Corporate Strategy Resources

Strategy Resource	1. Set up Strategy	2. Create Strategy	3. Alternative Strategy Analysis	4. Implement and Execute Strategy	5. Monitor, Evaluate and Revise	6. Revise as Needed
CEO	✓	✓	✓	✓	✓	✓
Board	✓	✓	✓	✓	✓	✓
HR Director	✓	✓	✓	✓	✓	✓
Strategy Director	✓	✓	✓	✓	✓	✓
Strategy Consultants	✓	✓	✓	✗	✗	✗
Executive Directors	✓	✓	✓	✓	✓	✓
Senior Management		✓	✓	✓	✓	✓
Business SMEs		✓	✓	✓	✓	✓
Consultants and Contractors (As required)		✓	✓	✓	✓	✓

Figure 19: *Resources for Corporate Strategy Management*

The human resource requirements for strategy projects will depend on the strategy phase and most of them will generally fall into three categories: in-house resources, contract staff from consulting firms, and contractors from recruitment agencies and other human resource (HR) providers.

There will always have to be a fine balance between internal and external resources in creating, analysing, and implementing the strategy.

Create a Strategy

This stage focuses on reviewing the past financial and non-financial performance and/or the current situation by using strategic tools and techniques such as Strengths, Weaknesses, Opportunities and Threats (SWOT) and the Boston Consulting Group (BCG) Matrix. (*Source: BCG.com and Corporatefinanceinstitute.com*)

The SWOT Analysis evaluates each business unit's performance, illustrating what worked well, what was successful, current and future customers, business challenges, who their competitors are, market analysis and information about the opportunities. (*Source: Corporatefinanceinstitute.com*)

Product strategies from the BCG Matrix include the following (*Source: BCG.com*):

- Stars – Invest through Market Penetration.
- Cash Cows – Invest through Market Penetration and Market Development.
- Question Marks – Invest through Market Penetration and Development.
- Dogs – Dispose or discontinue division.

The completion of SWOT Analysis, the BCG Matrix, and other relevant current types of analysis will lead to the setting up of business performance measurements for each business unit relating to the following categories:

- Liquidity or cash optimisation
- Debt management
- Market value and investment
- Mergers, acquisitions, and disposals
- Human Resources (HR)
- Technology (IT)
- Sales and marketing
- Customer services
- Metrics in other business units

Alternative Strategies

The main goal for this phase is to identify the alternative strategies that leverage the insights, consisting of the issues gathered from creating the strategy. "Evaluating the alternatives will involve their suitability, acceptability, and feasibility." (*Source: Johnson, G., and Scholes, K., 1997 – Johnson.dk*).

Below are the alternative strategies:

- Suitability addresses questions about opportunities and weaknesses.
- Acceptability considers expected performance outcomes.
- Feasibility determines if the company has the capital resources to fund the strategic changes. (*Source: Johnson, G., and Scholes, K., 1997 – Johnson.dk*)

Corporate Strategy Objectives

Strategic Category	Criteria	Business Objective	Priority	Execution
Financial	Perform Economic Profit (EP) for the Company	Discontinue products with negative EP	Medium	< 3 months
	Profitability	Improve Gross Profit, Net Profit, ROCE, and other	High	
	Liquidity Optimisation	Introduce more efficient credit control policies	High	
	Debt Management	Manage and stop accumulating further debt	High	< 12 months
	Market Value and Investment	Improve shareholder value	High	< 3 months
Stability	Strategy Development and Company Performance	Introduce agile lifecycle and value-based performance measurements	High	
	Talent, Organisational Structure, Leadership, Succession Planning, Training, Diversity and HR	Define culture, values and recruit suitable candidates	High	
	Regulation and Compliance	Comply with legal, regulation and Brexit	High	
	Cost of Sales and Cost Structure	Streamline cost structure linked to value-based strategy	High	
	Barriers to Entry	Identify barriers to enter new markets	Medium	
	Health, Safety, and Security	Introduce efficient health, safety, and security policies	High	
Competitive	Pricing Policy	Review and align with competitors	High	
	Product Range and Quality	Increase research and development	High	
	Use of Artificial Intelligence (AI)	Accurate analysis of internal and external factors	High	
	Technology, Systems, Digitisation and Processes	Improve technology and shorten product lifecycle	High	< 12 months
	Customer Acquisitions and Retentions	Market penetration and use of AI	High	< 3 months
Industry Position	Investor Relationships and Engagement	Shareholder engagement and requirements	High	
	Corporate, Social and Responsibility (CSR)	Invest in projects promoting CSR	Medium	
	Competition	Identify key competitors and realistic plans for growth	High	
	Risk and Growth	Positive EP as indicator for decision-making	Medium	
	Customer Service	Improve customer experience and reduce complaints	High	

Figure 20: *Example of Corporate Strategy Objectives and Requirements*

"Process mapping will enable the design of a value-based operating model that will link to strategy and incorporate structure, style, staff, skills, systems, and shared values." (*Source: Mckinsey.com*)

The recruitment strategy will attract a competent board, senior management, and a cross-functional workforce to support the corporate strategy. The organisational structure created, performance evaluations, rewards given, remuneration, and the culture must all be linked to supporting the corporate strategy.

The key outputs of choosing the right strategy will contribute to defining the company values, purpose, mission, and vision statement. This information will help shape the business's future direction, both in the short and long term. The main goal is to start by focusing on the organisation's purpose and values.

It's necessary now to concentrate on mission statement creation, which defines the company's existence and corporate objectives. The corporate mission outlines the resources needed to accomplish the short-term and long-term future direction.

The business objectives that have been shown in the above processes must align with the values, purpose, vision, and mission statement. The business objectives will be prioritised based on the corporate strategy, with the ranking of high, medium, and low, based on the risk management scoring system.

The next activity is to provide the detailed business unit level objectives linked to the corporate vision, mission, and business objectives to ensure that financial and non-financial goals are achieved.

Finally, completing the above process would involve performing a strategy value-based test and creating an implementation plan to execute the strategy. (*Source: Mckinsey.com*)

Implement and Execute Strategy

This phase involves reviewing the high-level corporate objectives and the detailed executable action plans, including the allocation of budgets for directing the company to implement its strategy. For strategy implementation to be executed successfully, this will involve the efficient management of people and processes.

"Rather than the traditional approach of having multiple business objectives being executed in a sequential timeline, **the Agile value-based corporate strategy delivery approach involves selecting a set of objectives from the strategic category to be executed incrementally with specific timelines prioritised by the organisation**" (*Source: Mckinsey.com*)

Strategic budget approval is required to ensure that the various business units and departments have sufficient resources to execute their strategy. Funding is critical because inadequate resources will result in a failure to execute the strategic plan. This process links the strategic budgets and strategic project plans to the values, purpose, mission, vision, corporate strategy, and business unit objectives.

In this stage, the goal is to build an organisation that can deliver changes by retaining competent and talented employees, sticking to the competitive operational models, and maintaining an efficient organisational structure.

Corporate Strategy Change and Implementation

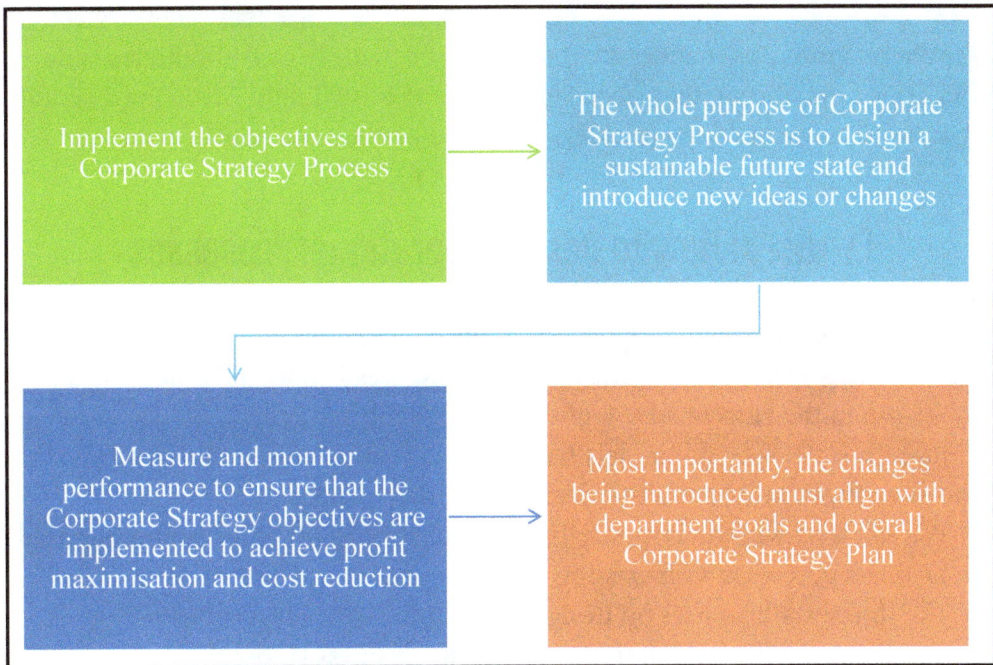

Figure 21: *Corporate Strategy Objectives for Implementation*

Monitor, Evaluate, and Revise

The next activity is to provide the detailed business unit level goals which are linked to the values, purpose, vision, mission, and high-level business objectives to ensure that value-based performance is achieved.

This phase focuses on reporting and risk management status updates to ensure that bottlenecks are removed, and necessary change is introduced to support the implementation or revision of the strategy. Additionally, this stage involves data analytics to monitor progress and identification of the root cause for failure or success in executing the required corporate strategy.

Revise as Required

The strategic review process is a continuous activity led by the CEO and supported by the Office of Strategy Management. The executive directors will hold regular meetings to check if the project plans and budgets align with the corporate strategy.

Where significant changes are required to be made because of internal and/or external factors, the strategy needs to be revised accordingly, involving a smaller set or larger number of stakeholders impacted by the revision.

EXERCISE 3: How to Design Operational Processes

This exercise concentrates on mapping business processes, which is what processes are widely known for. The approach involves simply documenting a process – both in the current state and defining the future state.

In each state, specific models have been carefully chosen to assist with that process analysis, measurements, design, and implementation.

We will start with definitions. The current state is about documenting modern business processes with existing problems and company structure.

The future state focuses on designing the future business processes by introducing recent changes and optimisation of the business landscape.

Operational Process Models for Current State Analysis

This is the best framework for starting any process project. The method focuses on process analysis by creating a central map that provides a holistic big-picture view.

Business Process Hierarchy and Levels

Level 0 – Company Wide
Level 1 – Business Unit
Level 2 – E2E Function
Level 3 – Main Process
Level 4 – Sub Process
Level 5 – Procedures and Work Instructions

Figure 22: *Business Process Levels for Organisations (Source: SAP.com)*

If this information is readily available, then it's better to optimise those hierarchies. Business process hierarchy is a valuable tool used to determine the activities performed in an organisation based on its myriad departments and functions.

The information is critical not only in business structure design but also for defining value-adding processes and linking them to the corporate strategy. Refer to chapter 1 for the definition of process hierarchy levels.

Company-wide Business Process Catalogue

Level 0 - Company Wide			
Level 1 **Business Unit**	**Level 2** **E2E Functional Process**	**Level 3** **Main Processes**	**Level 4** **Sub Processes**
1. Corporate Strategy	1.1 Business Strategy	Add As Required	Add As Required
	1.2 Relationship Management	Add As Required	Add As Required
	1.3 Additional Functions	Add As Required	Add As Required
2. Business Operations	2.1 Front Office	Add As Required	Add As Required
	2.2 Middle Office	Add As Required	Add As Required
	2.3 BackOffice	Add As Required	Add As Required
3. Shared Services Functions	3.1 Human Resources	Add As Required	Add As Required
	3.2 Information Technology	Add As Required	Add As Required
	3.3 Sales and Marketing	Add As Required	Add As Required
	3.4 Finance	Add As Required	Add As Required
	3.5 Additional Functions	Add As Required	Add As Required

Figure 23: *Company-wide Business Process Catalogue (Source: SAP.com)*

The model obtains output from the business process hierarchy levels by breaking down the processes performed in each department and function. This is a fundamental way to observe the volume of processes performed by those functions and the workload associated while completing those tasks.

It's also a great way to be able to determine the scope of the processes and check if you can get that end-to-end design. In most cases, listing the processes can be a fundamental method of discovering missing processes.

The volume of processes can also be an indicator of whether that business function contains excessive processes, and is, therefore, performing non-value-adding activities, or has too few operational processes which require further addition.

Business Process Ranking

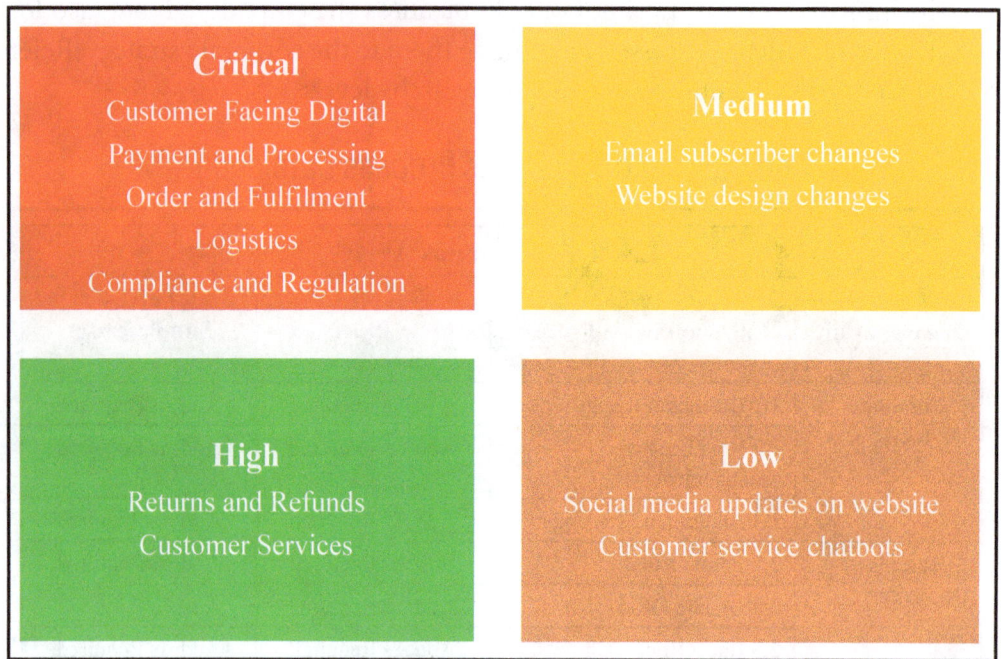

Critical Customer Facing Digital Payment and Processing Order and Fulfilment Logistics Compliance and Regulation	**Medium** Email subscriber changes Website design changes
High Returns and Refunds Customer Services	**Low** Social media updates on website Customer service chatbots

Figure 24: *Business Process Ranking Matrix*

Business process ranking is fundamental in defining the most important processes that must operate at optimal levels 24/7, 365 days a year. The ranking helps in deciding which processes need the quantum of investment.

Critical and high processes are the most value-adding ones from a customer standpoint in relation to health and safety, regulation, and compliance. If there is an issue with these processes, ideally it must be resolved within thirty minutes at the latest depending on the service level of agreement (SLA).

Medium and low-ranked processes are important but have specific service-level agreements to be resolved later within the agreed time frames because they are not critical for business operations.

Business Process SWOT Analysis

Strengths

Process weaknesses have been identified

Business process investment provided to address weaknesses and thread

Opportunities

Introduce new business processes to mitigate weaknesses and threats

Weaknesses

High cost to serve customers

Extensive manual procedures

Longer cycle times

Lack of data for process reporting

Threats

Revenue loss from dessatisfied Customers

New entrants with better customer service

Significant concern about the future

Figure 25: *SWOT Analysis Example (Source: Corporatefinanceinstitute.com)*

A business process SWOT Analysis model is a great process design methodology to determine the current state of the processes. It's simply a health check at the holistic level to determine what's working and what isn't.

The definition of SWOT Analysis is simple as enumerated below:

- Strengths: What is good about the company processes?
- Weaknesses: What are the high-level problems with the processes?

- Opportunities: What can be introduced for process improvements?
- Threats: What are the biggest risks affecting the processes?

RACI Matrix

Business Unit	Responsible	Accountable	Consult	Inform
Business Operations (Project Sponsor)		✔		
Business Operations	✔		✔	
Sales and Marketing			✔	
Customer Experience	✔		✔	
Digital Services	✔		✔	
Fulfilment	✔		✔	
Courier Services	✔		✔	
Business Excellence				✔

Figure 26: *RACI Matrix Example (Source: CIO.com)*

RACI is a great framework for allocating the roles, responsibilities, and ownership of a project. Its main objective is to confirm the business processes, departments, roles and responsibilities of cross-functional teams that bring about the change initiative.

The RACI acronym is broken down as the following:

- Responsible are stakeholders who perform and complete the process. This means that each process is assigned as R.
- Accountable (A) is the stakeholder that provides approval or final approval.

- Consult (C) is the stakeholder that provides input based on their subject matter of expertise level.
- Informed (I) are stakeholders that need to be updated on the project progress at specific milestones but are not necessarily involved in daily interactions.

SIPOC Framework

S Supplier	I Input	P Process	O Output	C Customer

Figure 27: *Business Process SIPOC Example (Source: Aris.com)*

This is a great framework to test if the processes are accurate and/or complete. The components act as controls for quality assurance. The framework can also be used as information that goes to define a process map. The categories are as follows:

Supplier

- Which systems provide information to trigger the process?
- What are internal functions and who are the external suppliers providing inputs into the process?

Inputs

- What is the system received data-specific data attributes?
- What are the manually entered data-specific attributes?

Process

- What are the steps or activities performed throughout the process?

Output

- What documents and artefacts are produced from the process?

Customer

- What internal and external stakeholders use the output being produced?

Process Workshop Interview Questions

- How would you describe the business process in the company?
- How has the business process benefitted the company?
- What value does the business process provide to customers?
- Does management contribute to the success of the business process?
- Who are the primary participants or stakeholders in the process?
- What are the triggering events for this business process?
- How could you describe the collaboration between the distinct functions?
- Are there any problems or barriers impacting success?
- What are the objectives of the business process?
- What requires the business process to be completed?
- Using the SIPOC framework, who supplies information into the process, what are the inputs, the steps, what is the main output or documents produced, and who are the main customers in the process?
- What improvements and opportunities would you like to see that can help in eliminating some of the problems on the process map?

Document Current State Business Process

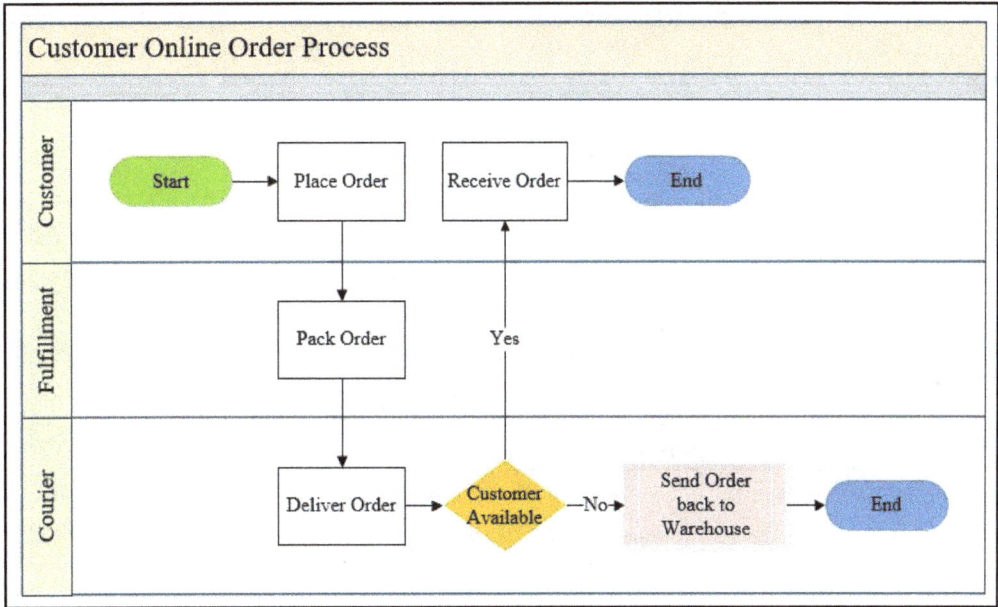

Figure 28: *Current State Process Maps*

Document Future State Business Process

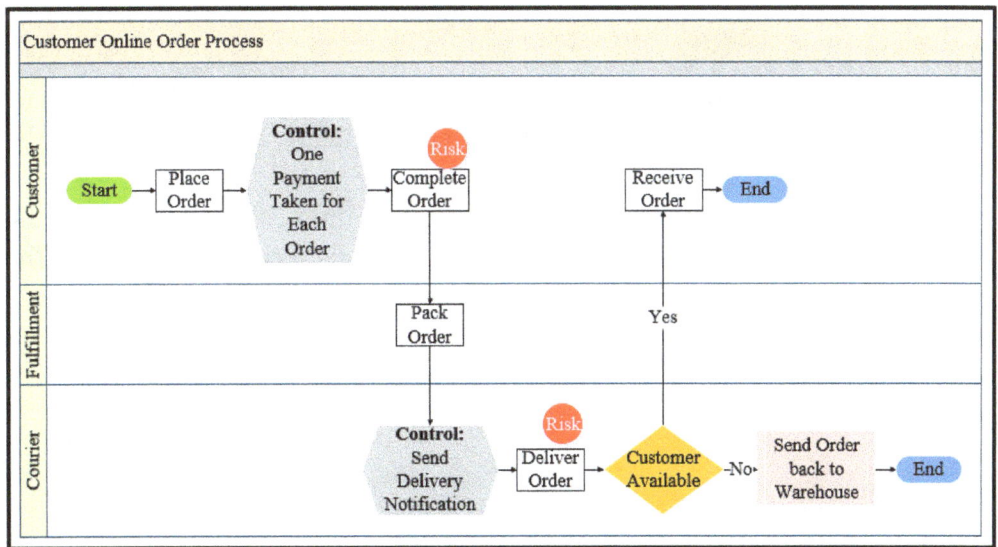

Figure 29: *Future State Process Map*

Future State Business Process Requirements

Business Unit	Priority	Description	Impact on Customer	Benefits
Digital - Website	Must Have	Provide website with high performance	• Loss of customer to alternative online and offline retailers • Loss of revenue from customers leaving to seek out other retail competitors	• Customer satisfaction • Customer retention • Increased revenue • Increased market growth • Industry leadership
Digital - Website	Must Have	Prevent pages from crashing when customer is shopping		
Digital - Website	Must Have	Provide functionality to ensure that customer is not charged twice for the same order		
Digital - Website	Must Have	Ensure that customer is provided order/payment confirmation upon completing order		
Logistics	Must Have	Ensure that customer is provided with first delivery notification when order is ready to be delivered		
Logistics	Must Have	Customer to be provided with delivery notifications from the courier regarding delivery (time, etc.)		

Figure 30: *Future State Business Requirements*

As you can see, the above requirements have been generated from the future state business process outlined in figure 29. The requirements, effectively, define the change that needs to be made to arrive at that future state.

The current state business process is a great framework to understand the currently available ways of working and the problems facing the business. The future state, on the other hand, looks at the changes that need to be made to fix the problems.

Business Process Priority Matrix

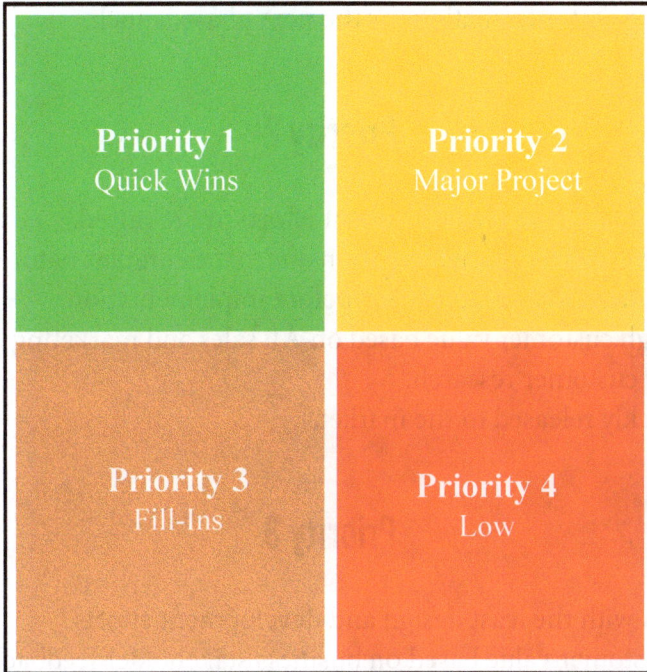

Figure 31: *Business Process Priority Matrix (Source: Productplan.com)*

This framework is especially important when choosing which improvements or changes need to be introduced to the process design.

Once the future state requirements have been gathered as part of the selection criteria marked by P1, P2, P3, and P4, this categorisation will help decide which changes are introduced first, second, parked for later, or never introduced at all because they don't provide any business value.

The priority level criteria are explained in more detail in terms of definitions and what is expected via priority implementation.

Priority 1

- Process features with the least design and development effort.
- Have the highest customer value based on marketing analysis.
- Contribute to the best customer journeys and experiences.

- Quick market release for customers to make purchases.
- More efficient learning curve in obtaining feedback from customers
- and using that information for the next phase launch.

Priority 2

- Complex design and development efforts are required.
- Excessive costs for implementation due to the complex nature of the change in being designed or developed before implementation.
- Have high customer value based on AI, sales and marketing research, and/or other customer research.
- Not quickly released to the market.

Priority 3

- Features with the least design and development efforts.
- Least customer value based on business stakeholder feedback.
- Not providing significant benefits that customers value.
- Quick release if capacity permits.

Priority 4

- Complex design and development efforts are required.
- Have low customer value based on AI, marketing, and other factors.
- No significant contribution to customer journey, experience, or satisfaction based on sales and marketing requirements.
- Not quickly released to the market.

Change and Implementation

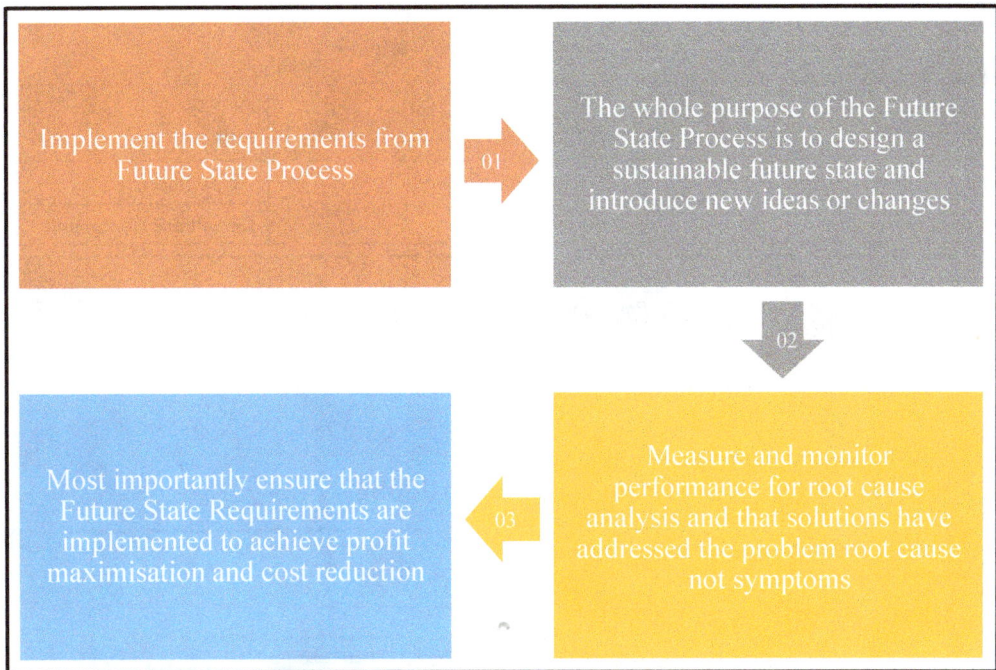

Figure 32: *Objectives for Future State Implementation*

Examples of Operational Process Maps Documented using VISIO

Company-wide Contact Centre Processes

This is the phone order and phone complaint process for a contact centre operation that has been documented using MS Visio BPMS.

MS Visio is one of the easiest and most user-friendly business process mapping tools in the market. There are free On-line Training courses available on the Microsoft website with materials that are easy to follow to help with your learning phase.

Company-wide Process Hierarchy

Level 0 – Company-wide			
Level 1 **Business Unit**	**Level 2** **E2E Functional Process**	**Level 3** **Main Process**	**Level 4** **Sub Process**
L1 – Operations	L2 – Contact Centre	L3 – Phone Customer Service	L4 – Phone Order
			L4 – Phone Complaint

Figure 33: *Company-wide Contact Centre Processes*

Phone Order Process

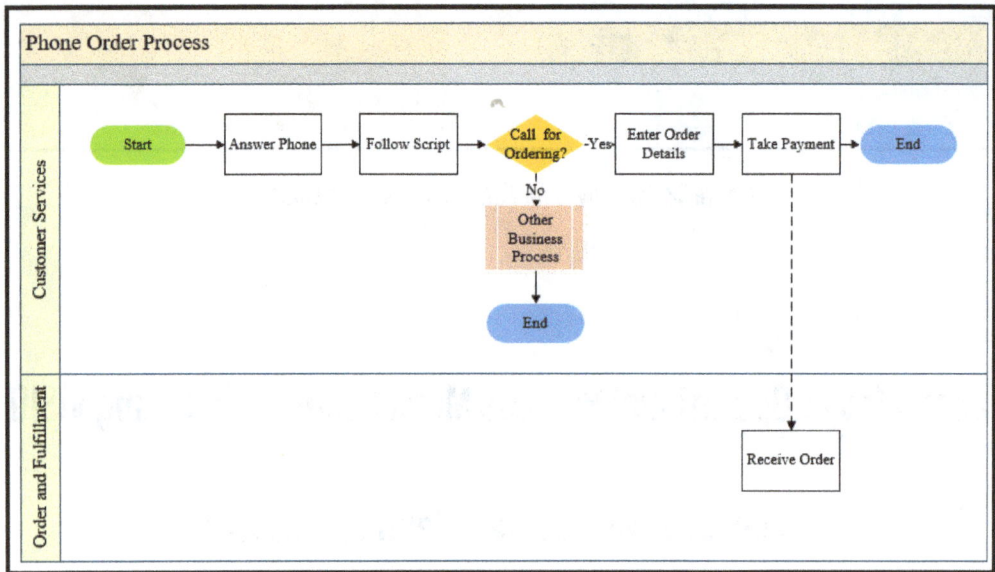

Figure 34: *Example of Phone Order Process (Software: Visio, Microsoft.com)*

Complaints Process

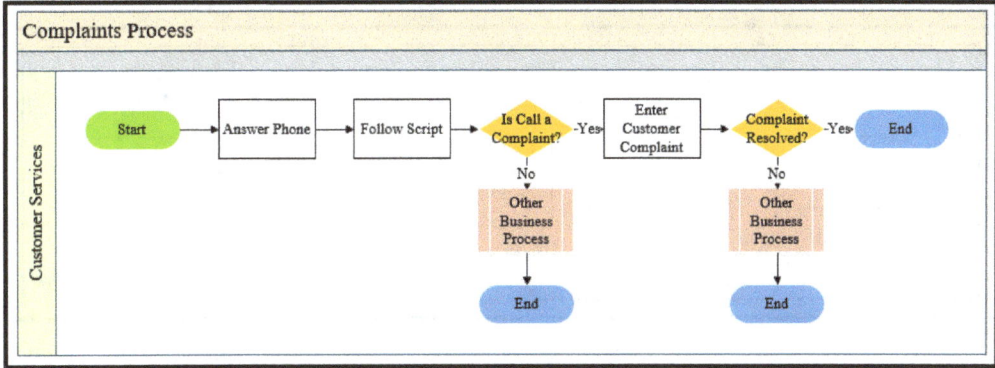

Figure 35: *Example of Phone Complaints Process (Software, Visio Microsoft.com)*

Examples of Operational Process Maps Documented Using Lucid Charts

Company-wide Marketing Campaign Processes

The Lucid Charts process map is one of the most user-friendly process mapping tools that you will find on the market. The design and navigation are exceptionally easy even without having any training and can be used by new beginners.

Company-wide Process Hierarchy

Level 0 – Company-wide			
Level 1 Business Unit	**Level 2 E2E Functional Process**	**Level 3 Main Process**	**Level 4 Sub Process**
L1 – Marketing	L2 – Campaign Management	L3 – Marketing Campaign Tracking	L4 – Marketing Campaign Analysis
			L4 – Measure On-line Marketing New Customer Acquisitions

Figure 36: *Company-wide Marketing Campaign Processes*

Marketing Campaign Analysis Process

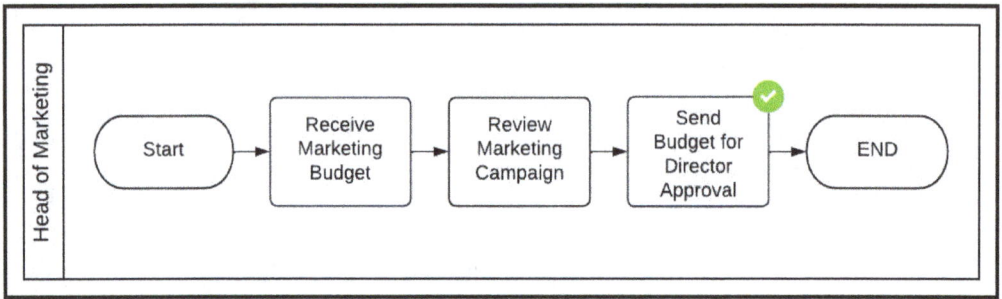

Figure 37: *Marketing Campaign Processes (Software: Lucid Charts)*

Measure Online New Customer Acquisition Process

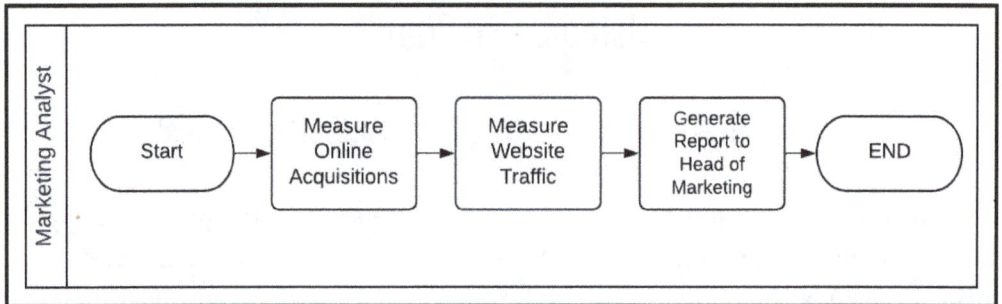

Figure 38: *Measure Online Customer Acquisitions Process (Software: Lucid Charts)*

Examples of Operational Process Maps Documented using ARIS

Company-wide Warehousing and Logistics Processes

I started using ARIS BPMN incredibly early in my career – around 2005 – and the BPMS is highly recommended as one of the industry-leading tools for documenting, storing data, and processing analysis. The benefits of BPMS are discussed in greater detail in chapter one of this process mapping guide.

Company-wide Process Hierarchy

Level 0 – Company-wide			
Level 1 **Business Unit**	**Level 2** **E2E Functional Process**	**Level 3** **Main Process**	**Level 4** **Sub Process**
L1 - Operations	L2 – Warehousing and Logistics	L3 - Fulfilment and Packaging	L4 - Pack Order
			L4 – Deliver Order

Figure 39: *Company-wide Warehousing and Logistics Processes*

Pack Order Process

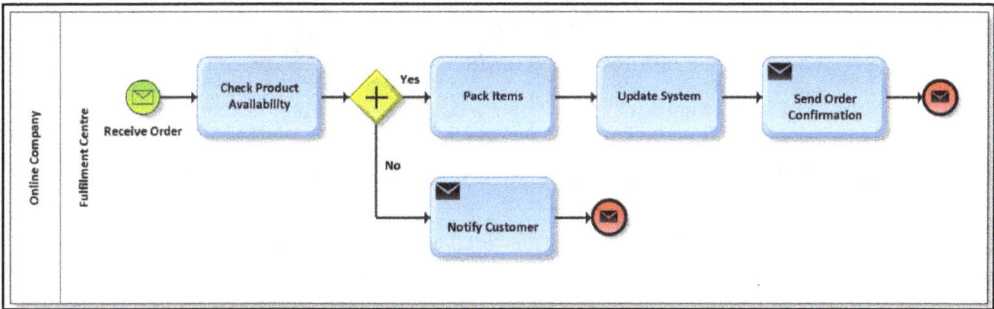

Figure 40: *Pack Order Process for Warehouse (Software: Aris.com)*

Deliver Order Process

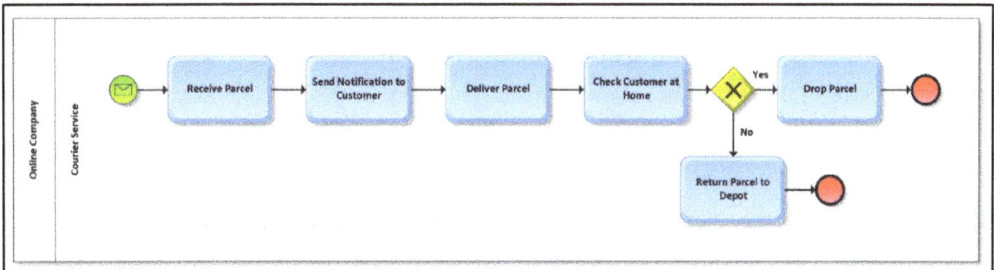

Figure 41: *Deliver Order and Parcel Process (Software: Aris.com)*

Examples of Operational Process Maps Documented Using Camunda

Company-wide Purchase-to-Pay Processes

I am new to using Camunda, and I would recommend the BPMN tool for easy-to-use functionality and process design templates. I did not have any previous training, but was able to quickly and professionally document the designed business process maps that have been presented in the illustration below:

Company-wide Process Hierarchy

Level 0 – Company-wide			
Level 1 Business Unit	**Level 2 E2E Functional Process**	**Level 3 Main Process**	**Level 4 Sub Process**
L1 – Finance	L2 – Financial Accounting	L3 – Accounts Payable	L4 – Create Purchase Order
			L4 – Approve Purchase Order

Figure 42: *Company-wide Purchase-to-Pay Processes*

Create Order Process

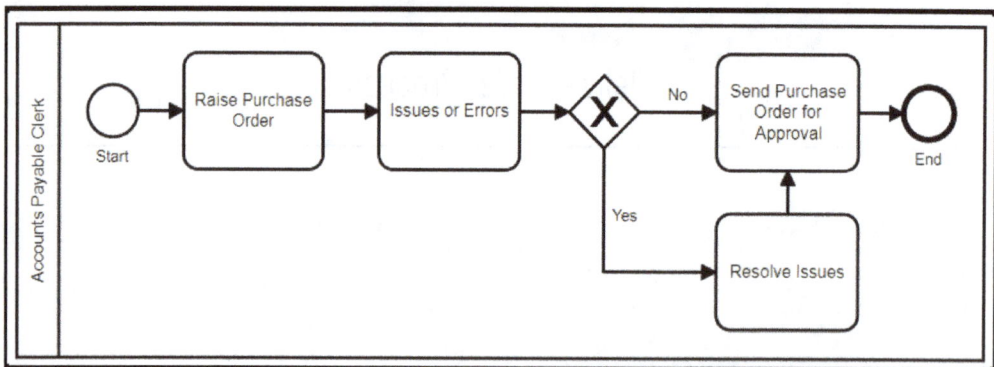

Figure 43: *Create Purchase Order Process (Software: Camunda.com)*

Approve Purchase Order Process

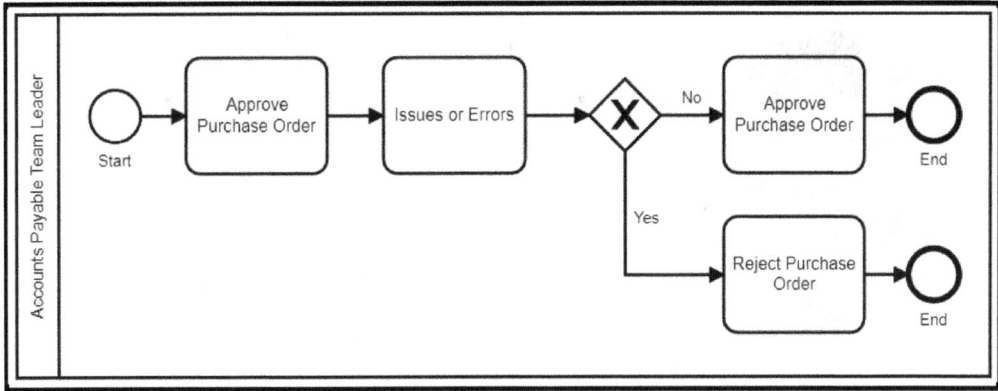

Figure 44: *Approve Order Process (Software: Camunda.com)*

Business Process Benchmarking with Competitors

The benchmarking being performed in this chapter is for electric vehicles from three of the world's most established brands in the industry. The goal is to show how quality processes are linked to customer satisfaction and experience.

To further demonstrate process quality, defects in the category selected and product recalls are connected to processes that have not completely achieved quality standards. The product is being recalled because customer requirements have not been fully implemented, therefore, impacting customer satisfaction.

Product recalls can be linked to health and safety standards not being met and they normally result in huge costs for reworks to be performed for replacing products.

Arguably, product recalls are linked to defective processes which have not followed the correct quality and assurance process standards for regulatory compliance and, most importantly, have not fulfilled customer expectations.

Business Process Benchmarking of Companies in the Automobile Sector

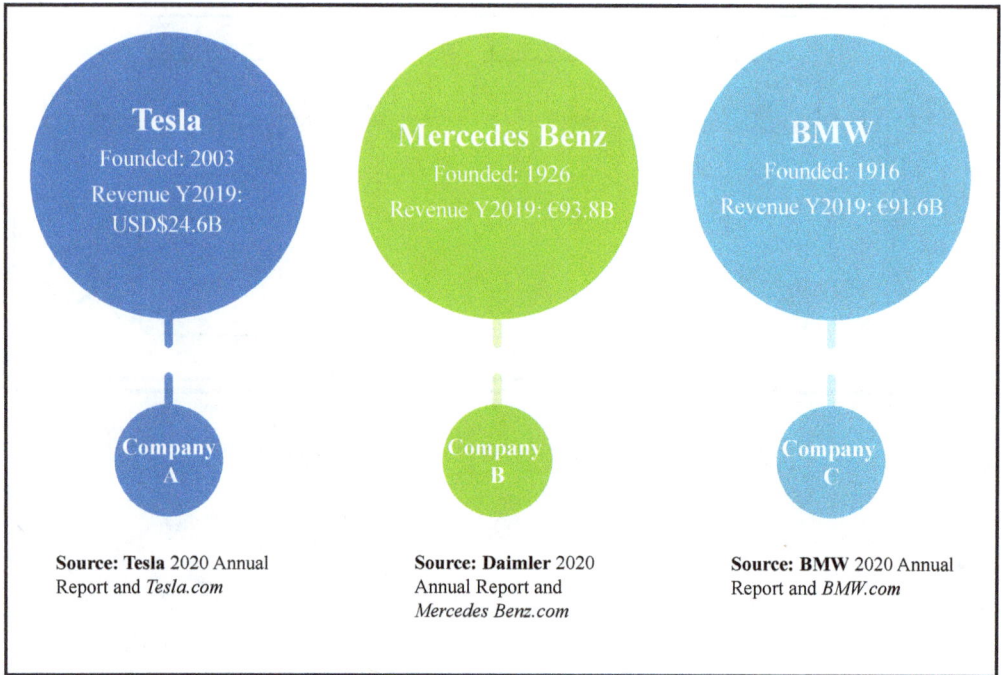

Figure 45: *Automobile Benchmarking with Competitors*

Tesla

Fuel Types: Electric Vehicles
Location of Production Plants: USA
Product Recalls: 158,000 (BBC News 2021)
Industry Awards: UK Car Award, 2020
Source: *Tesla.com, BBC News, Telegraph*

Mercedes-Benz Cars

Fuel Types: Electric Vehicles, Hybrid (Electric, Diesel or Petrol for longer distance)
Product Recalls: 1,292,258, 2021 (*BBC News*)
Location of Production Plants: Germany, Europe, Asia and South Africa

Industry Awards: Automotive Innovation Double Awards 2020
Source: *Mercedes-Benz.com, BBC News*

BMW

Fuel Types: Electric Vehicles, Diesel and Hybrid
Product Recalls: 26,700, 2020 (*BMWBlog.com*)
Location of Production Plants: Germany, USA and other parts of the world
Industry Awards: Multiple Awards 2020
Source: *BMWGroup.com, BMWBlog.com*

How Business Processes Contribute to Business Continuity

Business Process Management Model

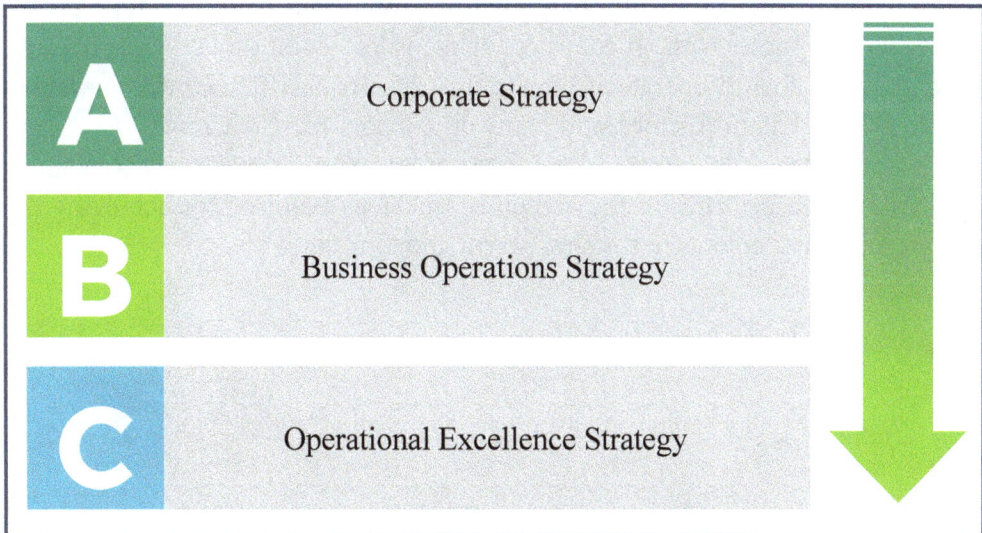

Figure 46: *Business Process Management and Operational Excellence*

Business process management contributes to business continuity by defining the activities required for the corporate strategy which focuses on the long-term operational strategy cantered around the short-term.

As we have seen in the previous pages of this chapter, process techniques have been applied to design corporate strategy through set-up, analysis, and execution.

The documentation of processes, policies, work instructions, working procedures, and the right system infrastructure is essential for business continuity in the post-COVID-19 world including implementing change quickly.

Business continuity ensures that the outlined roles and responsibilities can be performed by each function within the organisation.

Effectively, this is a great test because the trained employees can perform the required tasks using the process and procedure documentation.

The purpose of having efficient documentation is to ensure that day-to-day operations are not disrupted by unplanned events such as the COVID-19 pandemic, cyberattacks, weather disruptions, or other adverse events.

A robust business continuity plan with relevant documentation and systems can enable an organisation to make quality strategic decisions based on informed risk management assessment and risk management decision-making processes.

When lockdowns started being enforced in many countries around early March 2020, some businesses were able to continue operating at maximum capacity, and you will find that these companies had robust business continuity plans.

Other companies without contingency plans lost significant revenue because they were not able to operate at maximum capacity e.g., JC Penny, Norwegian Airline, Hertz, Latam Airlines, and many others. (*Source: CNN.com*)

Overall, processes are critical for the success and continuation of a business by defining and prioritising the activities, the steps required for achieving the goals, and measurements in the short-term and long-term phases.

Case Example

Vodafone: Boosting Agility, Transparency, and Scalability with Camunda (BPM – *Source: Camunda.com***)**

Background

Vodafone Germany is the largest national company in the Vodafone Group – one of the world's largest telecommunications groups, with 49.6 million mobile phone cards, almost 11 million broadband customers, and 14 million TV customers.

Vodafone employs 16,000 people in Germany and generates revenues of EUR 13 billion with a global workforce deployed across different countries and regions.

The company embarked on a business transformation programme to re-engineer its business processes using the Camunda Business Process Modelling Software. The goal was to establish an omnichannel end-to-end customer journey for improving their customer experience and generally, customer satisfaction.

Problems of not having Business Process Management

The requirement to set up the Camunda programme arose because the company was experiencing critical issues that were creating significant problems for its operational business and customer satisfaction.

The operating model and architecture landscape had legacy technology. It was inefficient because of the high maintenance and operating costs, a slow get-to-market for new products, and an inconsistent customer experience.

Business Process Re-engineering Methodology Deployed

The organisation had no centralised business process management system which resulted in the processes being stored in multiple locations and different tools.

Vodafone needed to allocate, identify and outline all the operational business processes and measure how the processes were performing before they could migrate the current state processes into the Camunda process software.

IT teams conducted process interviews with stakeholders from various business units. The goal was to understand exactly how each process worked from a business perspective and uncover hidden business processes that were not initially identified and possibly excluded from the business operating model.

Each business process was documented using the Camunda Modeler Software to provide visual diagrammatic standard maps of the business processes to enable business stakeholders to easily understand the information.

Financial & Other Benefits from Business Process Management

- Vodafone created a centralised business process management solution storing all migrated and documented business processes impacting customer experience, processes being used for analysis and KPI measurements.
- Identified all business processes and workflows impacting customer experience which were previously invisible (illustrating problems and suitable solutions aligning with the corporate strategy).
- Provided operational excellence, clear visibility, and end-to-end operational design across multiple functions as opposed to working in silos.
- Created best practice and standardisation in business process presentation by using BPMN methodology for business process mapping, primarily to help users of the processes easily understand the information documented.
- Streamlined operations by providing clarity on critical and value-adding processes and eliminating non-value processes that culminated in savings.
- Gave way to transparency, making it easy to manage the compliance and regulatory business processes necessary for adhering to the standards, policies, and statutory requirements. This shielded Vodafone from paying fines and compliance breaches through process risk mitigation techniques.
- Improved communications within business units through the infusion of clarity and accuracy in the activities performed within a function.
- Improved productivity and staff motivation by creating job standardisation and consistency in terms of training, inductions, and business procedures or work instructions across the organisation.
- Improved customer experience and satisfaction through business process monitoring and KPI process measurements.

- Optimised process KPI measurements to increase accurate understanding of operational issues and delivery of solutions that addressed the root cause of significant business problems as opposed to addressing the symptoms only.
- Improved the roles and responsibilities by using technology and re-engineered employees' activities resulting in reduced HR costs.
- Automated and optimised customer life cycles through the introduction of process management solutions that improved sales, customer service, experience, satisfaction, and retention.
- Automation also led to critical time savings in customer service, thereby freeing the employees to concentrate on other tasks that are more value-adding for the business and corporate strategy.

Summary

Documentation of process maps requires process-specialist knowledge to define the process framework and design artefacts at strategic and operational levels within the organisation. The process planning of work that needs to be performed must always factor in the high-level process analysis and the detailed process design.

Over the years, I have observed numerous projects that either disregarded processes in their entirety or performed the detailed design of documenting processes without that holistic overview necessary for accurately understating the hierarchy of main processes and measuring the value they provided for customer satisfaction.

Without this information, inaccurate decisions are bound to be made, impacting the delivery of projects, causing delays and resulting in customer needs remaining unaddressed mainly due to the lack of process information.

The application of the right models can make a significant difference between process maps adding value or having the opposite effect. Process mapping tends to quickly improve the inefficiencies by identifying processes using the Level 0-5 hierarchical models to achieve a high-level view or holistic landscape before documenting the details at operational levels.

This is followed by focusing on the high priority areas in applying process analysis and the application of other models such as SWOT analysis, process rankings, SIPOCs, current state, and future state process artefacts, and the other requirements that define the change for process improvement.

Depending on time scales and critical deadlines, process experts can choose the right models, analysis techniques, methodologies, and/or templates that will generate the maximum return on investment and this book has provided extensive examples in this chapter for achieving that goal.

Chapter Three

Risk and Internal Controls on Business Processes

Chapter Introduction

T HIS CHAPTER IS STRATEGICALLY linked to chapters one and two. While chapter one focuses on creating a process architecture, chapter two shows how strategy and operational processes can be documented. This chapter covers how risks and internal controls are critical to any business success and explains how companies can integrate processes for risk management.

Chapter three also recommends that risks and internal controls are added to the process maps. The concept is simple and can be executed through the identification of what can go wrong, which can be classified as risk identification, followed by the application of controls to mitigate or avoid such company risks.

Chapter Learning Outcomes

In this chapter, your main learning objectives will include:

- How process maps are used for risk management.
- Definitions of risk and internal control-related terminology.
- COSO framework and process management used for risk management.
- How to add internal controls on process maps to prevent risk from occurring.

- How to add risks to the process maps wherever identified.
- Examples of risk management frameworks and risk management models.
- How risk strategy is linked to corporate strategy.

The information provided in this chapter helps to confirm that end-to-end process maps can only be complete once the internal controls and risks have been added for achieving risk management purposes for that organisation.

Defining Risk and Internal Controls

There is a wider discussion about internal controls and risk management within every company. The audit committee, head of the internal audit, and risk functions are responsible for ensuring that all business units have adequate internal controls in place to mitigate any identified risk, including the documentation of business operational processes. (*Source: Coso.org.com*)

The identification and documentation of business process maps are vital to managing risks within an organisation. It is also exceedingly difficult to accurately manage risk without having a robust business process management software.

Risk management is extremely significant for any organisation to the point that the company's CEO, as part of the roles and responsibilities, is required to report any material identified risk to the audit committee and the board of directors.

The (COSO) framework is a process methodology created to help businesses address risk and control environments. The process methodology emphasises that the culture of risk is driven and enforced by the senior leadership team, then allowed to cascade to lower levels of the organisation. The management attitude towards risk defines the control environment of any trading business.

COSO's main purpose is to achieve operational effectiveness and efficiency, financial reporting reliability, and application of laws for regulatory compliance.

The COSO framework can be further enhanced by using process software which has the ability to link risks and internal controls added to the process maps.

COSO Framework

The COSO model has five main segments which include:

COSO Diagram Model

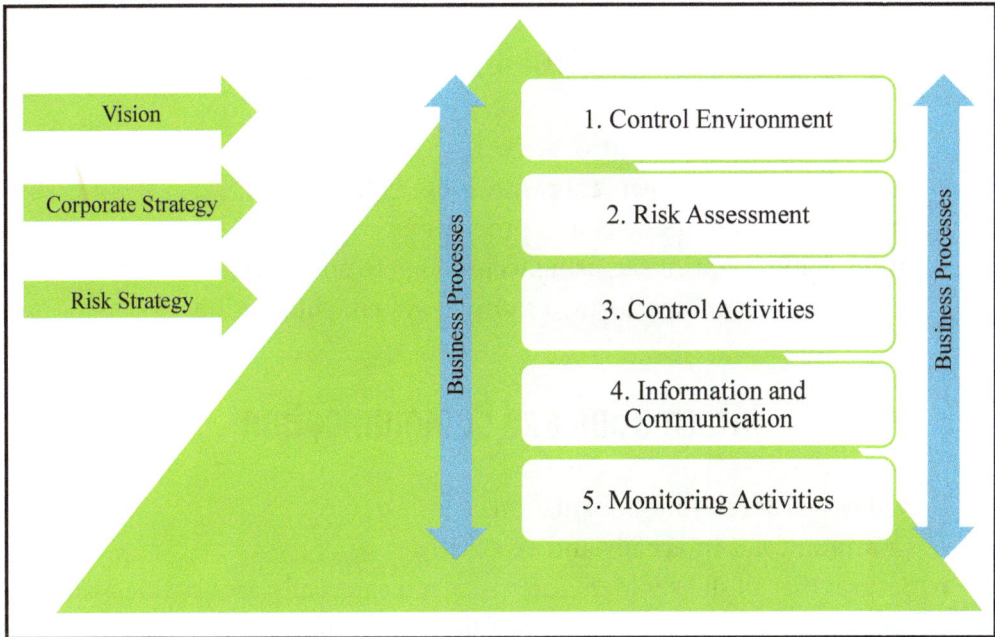

Figure 47: *COSO Company-wide Framework (Source: Deloitte.wsj.com)*

Control Environment

- Demonstrates commitment to integrity and ethical values.
- Exercises oversight responsibility.
- Establishes structure, authority, and responsibility.
- Demonstrates commitment to competence.
- Enforces accountability.

Risk Assessment

- Species-suitable objectives.
- Identifies and analyses risks.
- Assesses fraud risks.
- Identifies and analyses significant changes.

Control Activities

- Selects and develops control activities.
- Selects and develops general controls over technology.
- Deploys thorough policies and procedures.
- Automation is optimised using technology to ensure that control activities are not missed and performed through system automation.

Information and Communication

- Makes use of relevant information.
- Communicates internally and externally.
- Secures that all stakeholders, internally and externally, are provided with the right communication to ensure decisions and action items are not missed.

Monitoring Activities

- Conducts ongoing and/or separate evaluations.
- Evaluates and communicates deficiencies.

Although the COSO framework is a broader conversation that falls beyond this book's scope, it is essential to mention the connection between internal controls, risk models, and the application of process techniques for risk management.

Internal Controls on Business Process Mapping

Internal control is a mechanism used to detect and prevent risks or something undesirable from occurring. This can be a system-automated process or a manual procedure in the identified business process. The role is to detect and prevent risks from taking place at the same time.

"According to the Turnbull report, first published in 1999, defined internal controls and the scope is as follows: policies, processes, tasks, behaviour and other aspects of an organisation all combined." (*Source: Accaglobal.com*)

Internal control's basic purpose is to create touchpoints within a business process that can be documented, reviewed, and referenced to create accountability within the institution. The set-up of internal controls ensures that the business has a safe environment for the corporate objectives to be executed. Internal controls can be represented by internal milestones or external requirements outlined by the regulatory body. (*Source: Accaglobal.com*)

Performance process measurements and reporting will determine if the process is working effectively or if many things are going wrong, preventing company objectives from being achieved. In this scenario, a business process review enables management to have a holistic overview of the business processes that require re-engineering for continuous improvement.

To gain insight and accurate performance of a business process, asking the following three questions can assist with this analysis (*Source: reciricolcitylabs.com*):

- "What caused the event to occur", and what was the root of the problem?
- **"What process failed, allowing the event to occur", specifically outlining the steps of the business process?**
- "Is there a business policy that can be introduced to prevent recurrence"?

Internal controls can be effective, and below is a business process map showing the internal controls included. Though internal controls can solve significant business problems, they have limitations and cannot take care of every scenario.

Below are some common limitations to consider:

- Human error by a person involved in the internal control.
- Collusion between two or more parties aiming to override the function of the internal control.
- Management override, where senior leadership decides not to prioritise an area of internal controls and procedures.

- Eliminating segregation of duties where an individual can interfere with the whole or parts of internal controls.

Plotting Risks and Internal Controls on Business Process Mapping

This book specifically concerns risks and internal controls plotted on business process maps for managing and reducing risks.

The main types of enterprise risks usually consist of the following, either being strategic, financial, operational, or hazardous.

Though the board and audit committee are responsible for the reporting and management of company risk, each business unit is ultimately responsible for risk management in their individual areas.

Each function must have business processes and reporting metrics for the monitoring and management of things going wrong to ensure visibility and transparency of risk management and internal control effectiveness.

Risks and Internal Controls Plotted on Business Process Map

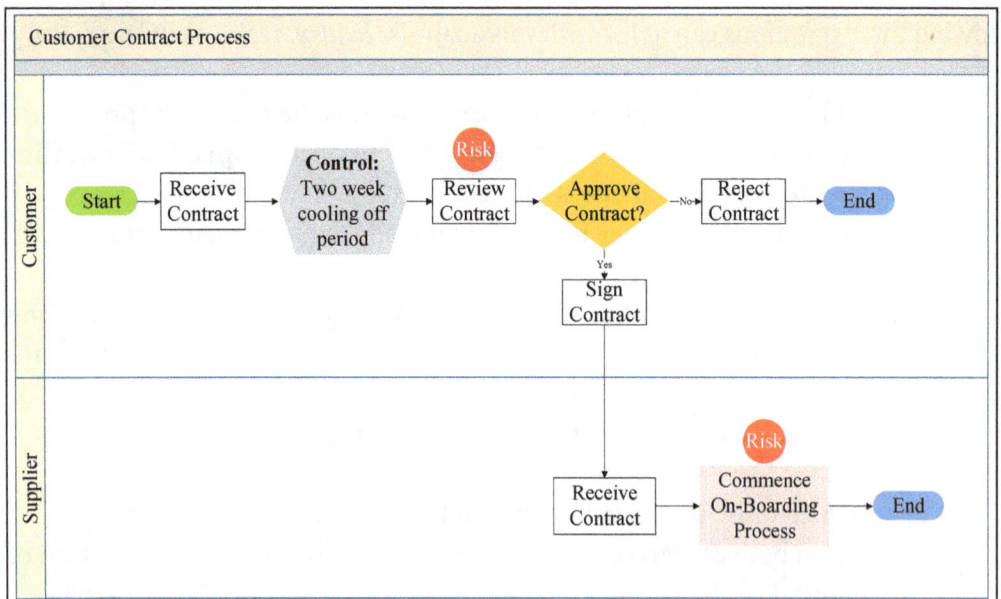

Figure 48: *Process Map with Internal Controls and Risk*

As you can see, in every annual report, there is a section about financial and business risks, which the CEO is responsible for reporting.

The reporting of any identified risk is strongly dependent on having automated processes set up on the system's internal controls, and business processes used as a tool in making these issues visible to management.

This is where the senior management is fully responsible for creating an environment and culture (expected behaviour from employees of that organisation) that promotes transparency in reporting risks.

The business processes must clearly show the internal controls, business policies, and the risks that have been identified. If a risk is classified as high impact and of high likelihood, one must take urgent action to address that risk. The risk management process for most companies looks quite similar, though there will always be variations such as the size, sector, and other multiple factors.

Risk Management Process

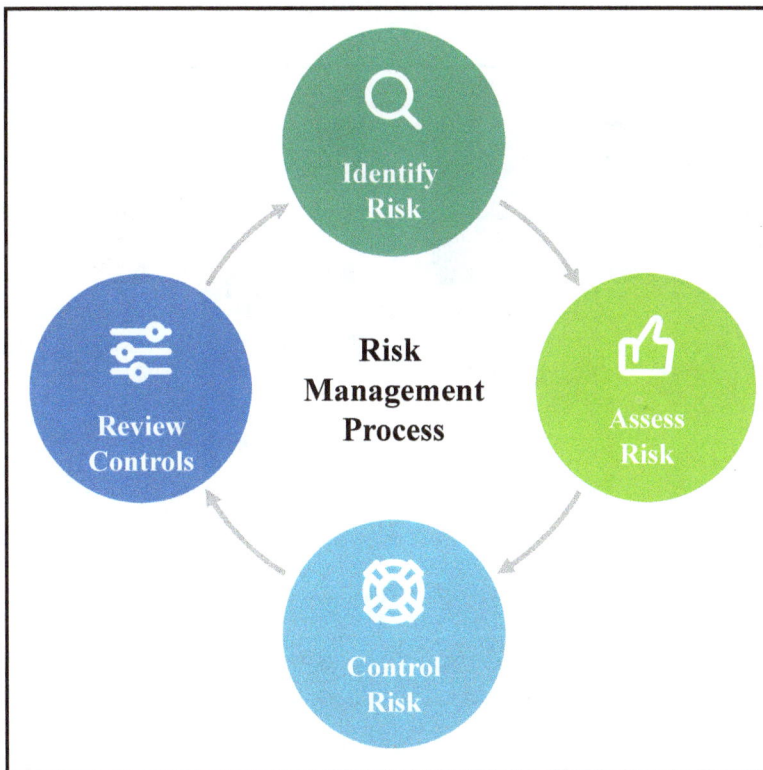

Figure 49: *Risk Company-wide Process*

Identify Risk

Document the risks and related events and bring together risk management-related data in a risk register that includes risk description, severity and impact, consequences, risk rating, mitigation plan, and related emerging issues.

Assess Risk

Assess and measure the identified risks using a set of criteria that includes impact, likelihood, controllability, and other determinants. Prioritise the risks and assist managers in determining which risks need to be addressed first. Having information about the severity and frequency is critical in deciding where the resources are going to be invested in that risk management.

Risk Management Model

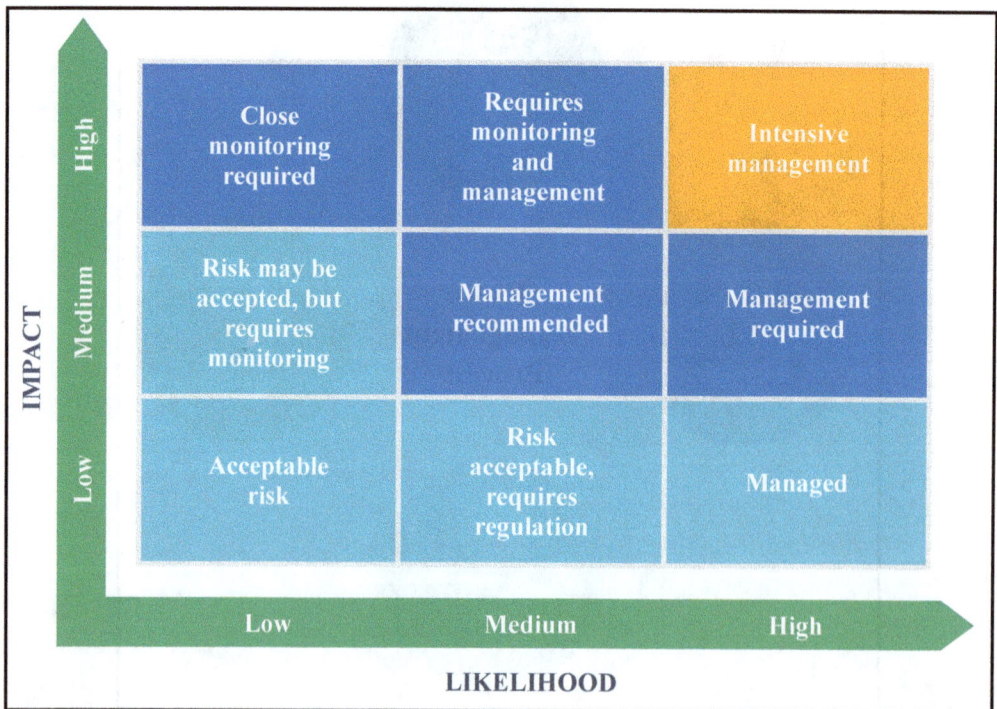

	Low	Medium	High
High	Close monitoring required	Requires monitoring and management	Intensive management
Medium	Risk may be accepted, but requires monitoring	Management recommended	Management required
Low	Acceptable risk	Risk acceptable, requires regulation	Managed

IMPACT (vertical axis) — LIKELIHOOD (horizontal axis)

Figure 50: *Company-wide Risk Impact Assessment*

Control Risk

Leverage established risk management frameworks to define a set of controls that mitigate such risks. Develop assessment plans to evaluate the effectiveness of the controls and assign them to owners based on roles and responsibilities.

Review Controls

Provide up to date information on risk management across the enterprise, including risk-control assessments, near-misses, remediation statuses, successes, failures, and trends. Drill down at the finer levels of detail on specific risks.

Risk Processes Benchmarking with Competitors

Competitor Process Benchmarking

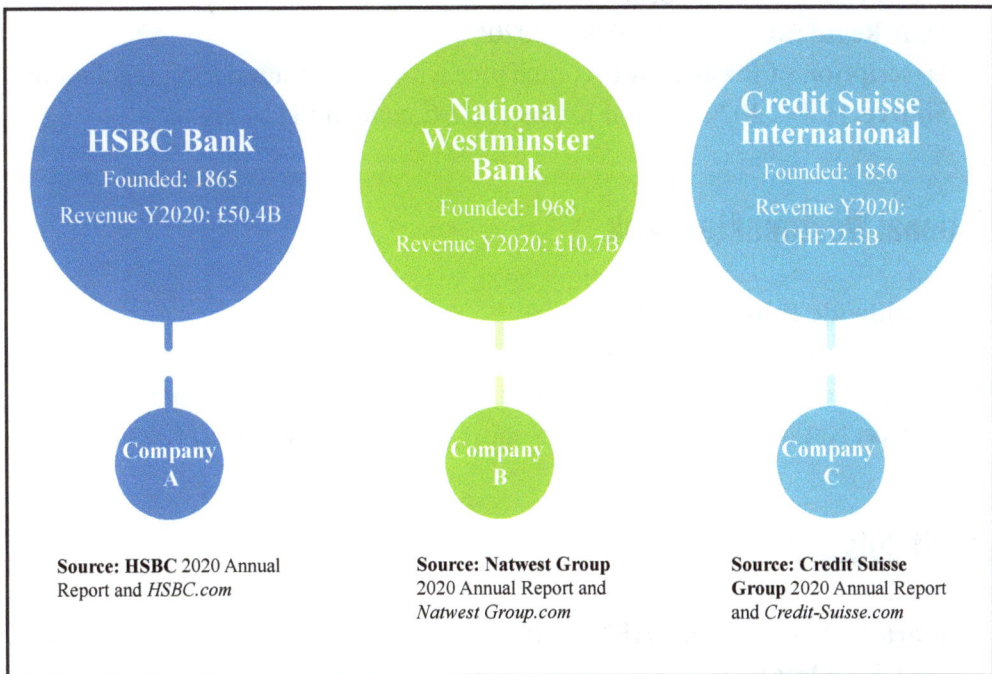

HSBC Bank
Founded: 1865
Revenue Y2020: £50.4B

National Westminster Bank
Founded: 1968
Revenue Y2020: £10.7B

Credit Suisse International
Founded: 1856
Revenue Y2020: CHF22.3B

Company A

Company B

Company C

Source: HSBC 2020 Annual Report and *HSBC.com*

Source: Natwest Group 2020 Annual Report and *Natwest Group.com*

Source: Credit Suisse Group 2020 Annual Report and *Credit-Suisse.com*

Figure 51: *Banks Compliance Risk Benchmarking*

In 2021, according to the Financial Conduct Authority (FCA), HSBC, National Westminster Bank, Credit Suisse, and many other banks breached significant regulations which resulted in combined fines of £567M. (*Source: FSA.org.uk*)

Irrespective of the background of issues in these banks, risks existed because processes were not managed effectively and were the potential root cause of the problem. Their risk management frameworks were not able to identify, manage, communicate, determine the impact, or comply with the required regulations. This is why these financial institutions failed to introduce new controls to their business operations in the realm of risk monitoring, reporting, and measurement activities.

Below are the fines and penalties charged against the three banks, and as you can see, the amounts are material costs that will impact their financial statements negatively by reducing their profit margins.

Having robust risk management processes in place and a controlled environment of risk transparency has the potential to mitigate these huge fines.

HSBC

Worldwide Revenue: £50.4B 2020
FCA Regulatory Fines: £63.9M 2020
Description of Breach: Non-compliance with money laundering regulations
Source: HSBC 2020 Annual Report, *HSBC.com* and *FCA.org.uk*

National Westminster Bank

Worldwide Revenue: £10.7B 2020
FCA Regulatory Fines: £264.7M 2020
Description of Breach: Non-compliance with money laundering regulations
Source: NatWest Group Annual Report, *NatwestGroup.com*, *FCA.org.uk*

Credit Suisse Bank

Worldwide Revenue: CHF22.3 2020
FCA Regulatory Fines: £147.1M 2020
Description of Breach: Non-compliance financial crime and anti-bribery
Source: *FCA.org.uk*

How Risk Management Processes Contribute to Business Continuity

Risk Management Model

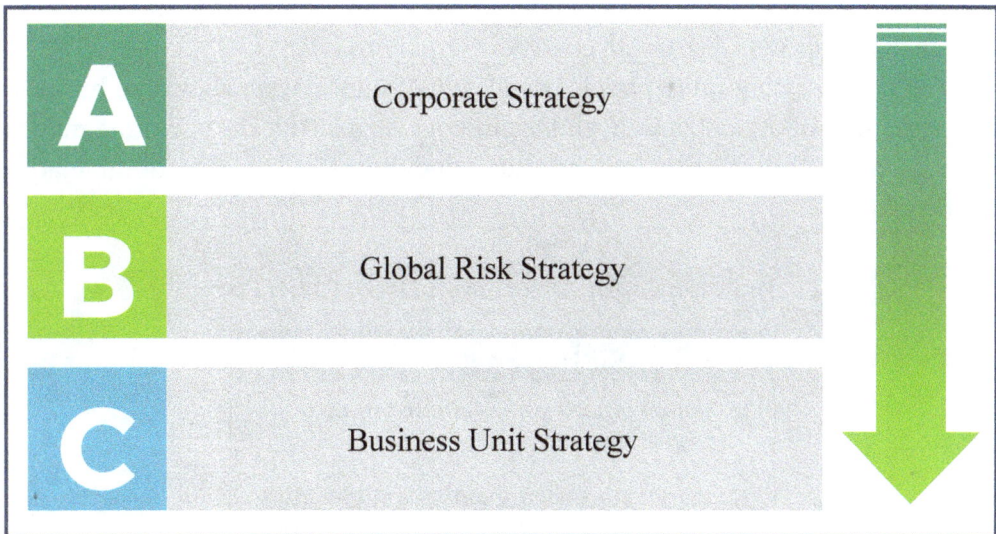

Figure 52: *Risk Strategy linked to Corporate Strategy*

The risk classifications vary depending on the enterprise, but the main types usually include the following: strategic, financial, economic, operational, compliance and regulatory, reputation, competition and security, fraud, and many other categories.

As you can see, as the risks defined impact all the company's business units, from a holistic level, the risk process, therefore, should be overseen by the Audit Committee and Internal Audit, scrutinising each business function accordingly.

There must be robust and updated processes to identify, report, assess, and take corrective action in mitigating risks based on their criticality and impact.

Even though the risks being mitigated should ideally align with the corporate strategy, the reality, is that there is usually a gap and misallocation of resources.

Efficiently managing a company's risks with business continuity may require integrating the systems to achieve a consistent and accurate view.

Enterprise risk management is concerned with strategic, financial, personnel, market, technology, business process-related, legal, geopolitical, regulatory, and environmental issues. Overall, the company-wide main concerns are usually connected to the factors of revenue, profitability, and customer satisfaction.

Business continuity focuses on the effects that would prevent an organisation from performing day-to-day operations such as processes, procedures, technology, system infrastructure, equipment, facilities, and people. (*Source: Riskmanagermonitor.com*)

The main goal of risk management is to protect the company from severe consequences or business disruption caused by unplanned events.

The business continuity plan is useful only if information about the business processes, organisational design, and technology aligns with the operating model. If there is a gap, then the plan loses relevance and there is a dwindling of value-adding benefits.

Risk Management Post-COVID-19 Crisis

TOP RISKS FOR 2021

1. Impact of pandemic-related policies and regulation on business performance

2. Impact of economic conditions on growth

3. Pressure of pandemic-related market conditions on demand

4. Adoption of digital technologies may require new skills that are in short supply

5. Privacy, identity management and information security challenges

6. Cyber threats

7. Impact of regulatory change and scrutiny on operational resilience, products and services

8. Leadership succession challenges; ability to attract and retain top talent

9. Resistance to change operations and the business model

10. Ability to compete with "born digital" and other competitors

Figure 53: *Business Continuity for Risk Management (Source: Protiviti.com)*

The risk assessment of business processes is critical to determine which processes are the most important, vulnerable, impactful, and dependent on the departments and functions which can be performed by using a SWOT Analysis.

Companies that prioritise business continuity as a substantial risk and invest in ensuring accurate documentation and updates are usually able to adapt their businesses during a crisis. An example would be global banks with advanced technology and infrastructure.

The combination of risk management and business continuity can potentially provide the resilience a company needs for transition and maximising its capacity to prepare for the unforeseeable.

Case Example

The Decline of Enron (*Investopedia.com*)

"Enron's highest shares were worth at $90.75 just before the company declared bankruptcy on Dec. 2, 2001, when the shares declined at $0.26."

Critical Problems

- Enron's leadership committed crimes by not adhering to regulations, making false accounting processes, and removing off-the-books accounting practices. (*Investopedia.com*). There were no internal financial controls to mitigate the financial risk associated with fraud and poor ethics by the senior leadership teams led to countless crimes.
- Enron followed accounting practices that did not align with the accounting disclosure standards of hiding debt and toxic assets from investors and creditors. They paid their creditors more than $21.7 billion from 2004 to 2011 (*Investopedia.com*).

Enron's Timeline

Year	Event
1985	Enron was formed after the merger of Houston Natural Gas Co. and Inter North Inc.
1995	Named "America's Most Innovative Company" by Fortune. The firm also goes on to win this award for six consecutive years.
1998	Andrew Fastow is promoted to CFO, and he ultimately spearheads the creation of a network of companies that hide Enron's losses.
2000	Enron's shares skyrocket to an all-time high of $90.56.
Feb. 12, 2001	Jeffrey Skilling replaces Kenneth Lay as CEO. However, Lay remains a member of the board of directors.
Aug. 14, 2001	Skilling resigns suddenly, and Lay takes over once again. Enron's broadband division also reports a massive $137 million loss. Analysts became wary of the company and subsequently dropped their ratings for Enron's stock. This in turn reduced the company's share price to $39.95, a 52-week low.
Oct. 12, 2001	Arthur Andersen's legal counsel instructs auditors to destroy all Enron files, except its most basic documents.
Oct. 16, 2001	Enron reports a $618 million loss, and a $1.2 billion value was written off. Stocks drop further to $38.84.
Oct. 22, 2001	Announces that the company is facing an SEC probe. Shares fall to around $20.75 that day following the announcement.
Nov. 8, 2001	Admits that the company has been inflating its income by around $586 million since 1997.
Nov. 29, 2001	Arthur Andersen becomes another casualty of the Enron scandal as the SEC expands its investigation.
Jan. 9, 2002	Justice Department launches a criminal investigation.
Jan. 15, 2002	Suspended from the NYSE.
June 15, 2002	Enron's accounting firm, Arthur Andersen, is convicted of obstructing justice.

Figure 54: *Enron Timeline (Source: Investopedia.com)*

New Regulations Created After Scandal

"Enron's collapse and the adverse fiscal impact on its shareholders and employees led to new regulations and legislation being created. The goal was to promote financial reporting accuracy for publicly held companies trading on stock exchanges. In July 2002, the Sarbanes-Oxley Act legislation was introduced and signed off by President George W Bush" (*Source: Investopedia.com*).

Summary

This chapter has effectively demonstrated that process management provides a significant contribution to risk management in identifying risk, evaluating the impact of that risk, and making decisions about how to address that risk.

The COSO framework is an industry-standard methodology for creating more transparent risk reporting as part of the company culture.

The examples in process benchmarking and the case example further explain that failing to embed process management in risk management models is the biggest risk any company can take because they will not be able to monitor risks effectively.

This is the reason companies are fined because risks are not accurately identified and evaluated in terms of the fiscal impact. The outcome of fines can significantly impact the company's going concern or have material liabilities on their financial statements. Such examples include companies ceasing to exist – like Enron in 2001 – and banks fined for not complying with relevant regulations in 2021.

Chapter Four

Business Process Improvement Models

Chapter Introduction

Pᴿᴼᶜᴱˢˢ ᴹᴬᴾᴾᴵᴺᴳ ᵁˢᵁᴬᴸᴸʸ involves the application of specific process improvement models, which aim to create a governed structure for simplifying the process analysis that needs to be performed.

Multiple industry-standard models that are recognised can be used globally to facilitate the analysis and evaluation of business processes.

The assumption being made here is that without the application of industry-standard models, it would be extremely difficult for organisations to set up their process architectures, document them, and gather information efficiently. The process models thus guide those performing process analytical activities.

Chapter Learning Outcomes

The main objective of this chapter is to cover the following topics:

- Definition of business process improvement.
- Examples of business process improvement models, which include Six Sigma, lean fabricating, Lean Six Sigma, total quality management, Toyota system production/just in time, and theory of constraints.
- How the centre of excellence strategy is linked to corporate strategy.

- How process improvement techniques contribute to increasing customer satisfaction and reducing operational costs.

Many publications and training courses provide the best practices for process improvement. It's extremely important to mention that choosing the most suitable process model is critical for process success in addressing the root cause of problems rather than highlighting the symptoms in your organisation.

Definition of Process Improvement

Business processes are considered a method of measuring efficiency, and most businesses must evaluate their techniques on a regular basis. Process improvement mainly involves business practices to identify, analyse, and improve the existing business processes or future state business processes.

The bid to optimise performance must always start with applying basic practice standards. It simply means that companies can transform business operations by improving quality services for their employees and customers. (*Source: Akintoye, Goulding & Zawdie, 2012*). Terminologies such as BPI (business process improvement) and BPM (business process management) all address business process improvement principles. Process improvement aims to minimise errors, reduce waste and defects, streamline operations, and even increase productivity throughout the organisation.

"Process improvement is mainly performed to set the standards for quality and customer experience. It involves a systematic approach that follows a particular method and sequence of tasks; however, it can consider different approaches too. Some examples of process improvements include lean manufacturing or even benchmarking which are different methods." (*Source: Coggin, 2018*).

When deployed successfully, process improvement results can be measured by metrics like customer satisfaction, customer experience, customer loyalty, product quality, productivity, and product delivery to customers.

Process improvement contributes to the development of employees, and increases profit and efficiency, leading to a higher ROI (return on investment). Aside from the named business process benefits, process improvement is part of the main feature of the BPM software.

Business Process Mapping Models

There are multiple industry-standard process mapping models, but the book has focused on talking about the following:

- Six Sigma: A data-driven process technique to reduce inefficiencies and improve the future process through process changes and measurements.
- Lean Fabricating: Focuses on creating robust processes by decreasing waste, therefore achieving profitability.
- Lean Six Sigma: A combination of Lean Manufacturing and Six Sigma principles to improve business performance.
- Total Quality Management (TQM): Incorporates stakeholders providing constant inputs to generate quality improvements.
- Toyota System Production/Just-in-time: This methodology concentrates on decreasing stock costs and having items just as they are required.
- Theory of Constraints: A precise process focused on finding and eliminating limitations and bottlenecks to achieve greater operational performance.

Process analysts assess and create processes for increasing profitability and scaling their business. Proper assessment of business processes requires understanding the root cause of the problems and improving the future state processes.

Depending on the complexity and urgency, the business can decide which process methodology is most suitable and can be sustained in the short to long term.

Six Sigma

Six Sigma was initially started at Motorola in 1986 by American engineer Bill Smith. The process framework was further developed by CEO Jack Welsch at General Electric in 1995 who incorporated it into their operating model.

Since then, process techniques have been used broadly for improving strategic, tactical, and operational performance. Six Sigma process methodology helps companies estimate process defects by creating continuous improvements to generate quality and, by measuring performance, to ensure that the root cause of problems has been addressed. (*Source: Aris.com*).

Six Sigma Framework

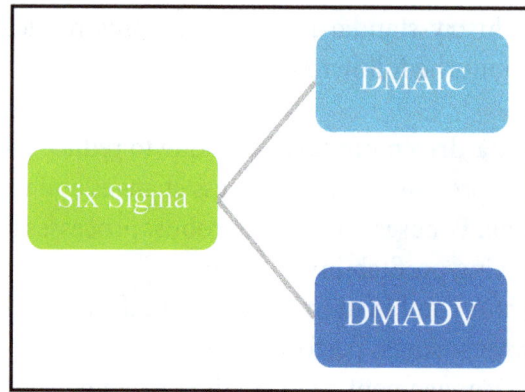

Figure 55: *Six Sigma Sub Frameworks (Source: Processexam.com)*

The benefits associated with applying the Six Sigma framework include:

- Process improvement.
- Defect and waste reduction.
- Improved productivity and cycle times.
- Reduced operational costs.
- Increased revenue through customer satisfaction.
- Increased margins and profitability.

Inside Six Sigma, analysts can choose from two of the methodologies: DMAIC for improving an existing process and DMADV for creating a new process.

Both frameworks apply value-adding principles which focus on data-gathering to accurately understand the root cause of problems and for designing the future state.

DMAIC Framework

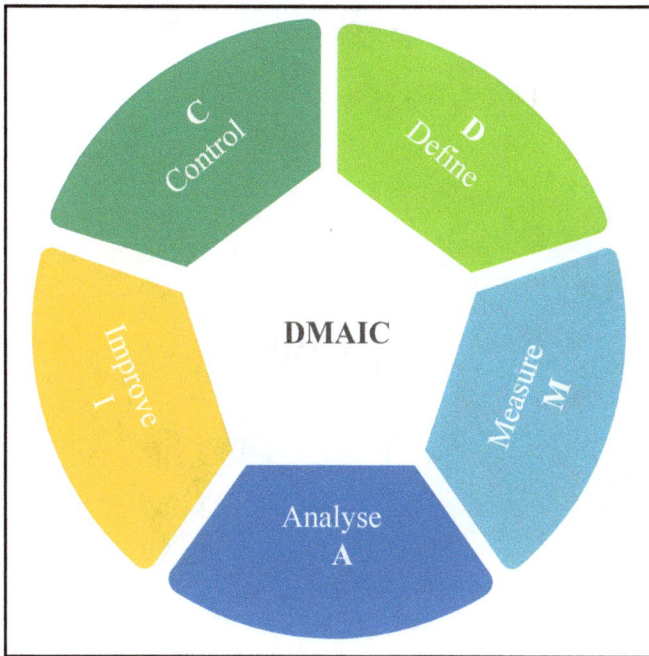

Figure 56: *DMAIC Model*

DMAIC usually follows these steps: (*Source: CIO.com*)

- Define the problem in the current process and obtain customer requirements.
- Measure the process using data analytics and performance metrics.
- Analyse to understand the root cause of problems and drivers.
- Improve the future process and performance metrics.
- Control the improved process and future process by addressing any deviations before they bring about the problems identified.
- Perform consistent and continuous quality improvement from the entire organisation, particularly starting with senior management, cascaded further to lower levels of the operating workforce.

DMADV Framework

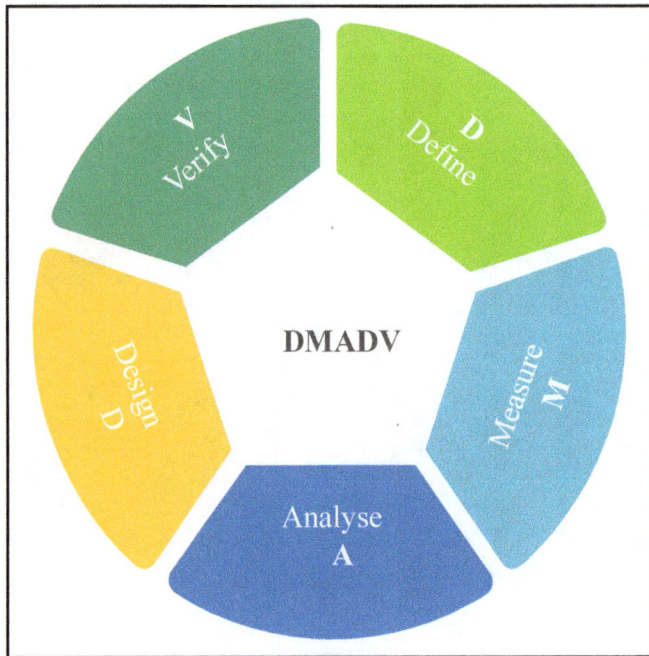

Figure 57: *DMADV Model*

DMAIC analysis models include the below:

- Fishbone or Ishikawa diagram
- Five Whys and Cost-benefit analysis
- Root cause analysis
- SIPOC (Suppliers, Inputs, Process, Outputs, and Customers)

DMADV follows comparable advances; however, businesses will review various components since a process does not exist or has been created.
The process stages on the DMADV Model are as follows:

- Define the process objective, including enterprise system and requirements.
- Measure the elements that are critical to quality (called CTQs).
- Analyse the activities on the process and provide improvement alternatives.
- Design the activities for process optimisation.
- Verify that the plan meets measure objectives and business needs.

Some companies do not have documented processes or business procedures on their operating models, which can result in a lack of understanding and miscommunications between multiple business units.

Simultaneously, numerous quality issues arise because employees perform similar tasks differently, mostly impacting the product design and service quality.

DMADV can be seen as a great opportunity to document the processes from scratch, measure the defects and grasp the root cause of problems on the process.

Six Sigma depends on data analysis and insights to accurately depict the problem. Using DMAIC and DMADV will enable the organisation to experience cost reduction, increased returns, and continuous improvement opportunities.

Fishbone Diagram for DMAIC and DMADV

This is a Six Sigma diagram, and the objective is to find out the root cause of problems resulting from identifying defects in the process.

Resembling a fishbone, the top of the outline expresses the category of the issue.

The lines branch out into various classifications of root causes based on the criteria outlined by the business performing the measurements.

Fishbone Diagram

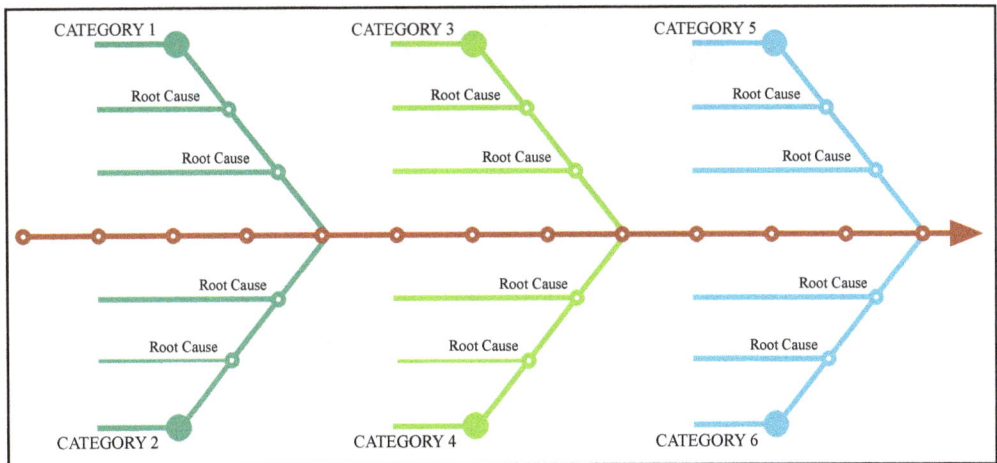

Figure 58: *Fishbone Diagram Lean Manufacturing*

Lean Manufacturing Types of Waste

"Lean Manufacturing's principles were introduced and have been extracted from Toyota, The Toyota Production System (TPS). The Lean strategy is focused on continuous incremental improvements on products and services while eliminating non-value-adding or redundant activities." (*Source: Toyota.com*)

"Lean is seen, as described by James Womack and Daniel Jones, to consist of five key principles: value by specific product, identify the value stream for each product, make value flow without interruptions, let customer pull value from the producer, and pursue perfection." (*Source: Womack and Jones, 1996, p. 10*).

Lean Waste

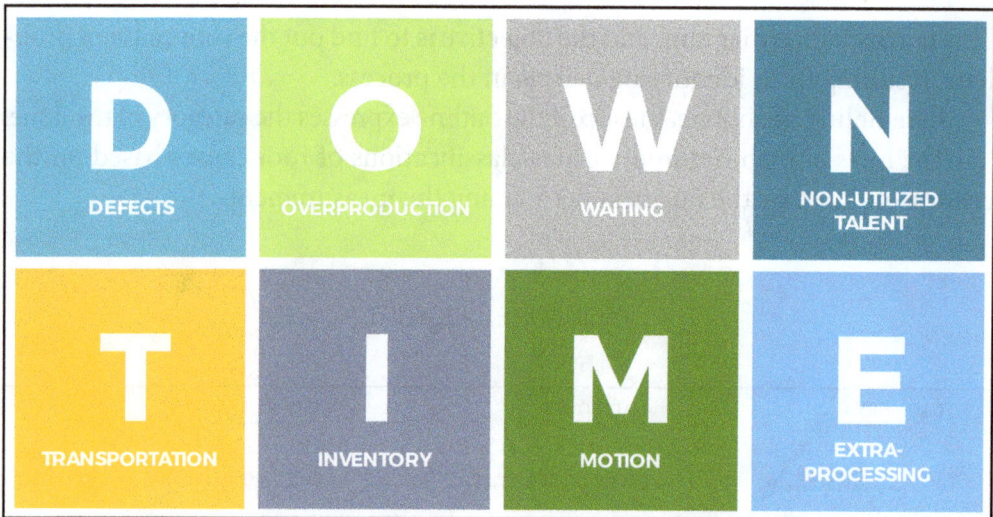

Figure 59: *Lean Manufacturing Eight Types of Waste*

Any activity that does not include esteem or is not needed to feature a strategy or guideline is a waste. (*Leanproduction.com*)

Waste can include:

- Defects: Rework time that is not adding value or producing anything.
- Overproduction: Creation of products not requested by the customer that can lead to misuse of space and overproduction.

96

- Waiting: Idle time that leads to waste.
- Skills: Involves under-utilisation of employees' skills, knowledge, and abilities that could otherwise increase productivity.
- Transportation: Unnecessary movement of raw materials, including people, moving those materials, and poorly planned trips.
- Inventory: Excess materials or materials not needed for current requests.
- Motion: Movements not adding value (e.g., people/machine movements) borne of inefficiency and resulting in waste.
- Over-processing: Extra work being performed that does not add value to improving or increasing productivity.

Charts for Lean Manufacturing

Insights and data analytics can be used in Lean Manufacturing to accurately depict the types of waste that the company needs to resolve.

Charts and graphs can be created to measure that performance metric. They are dependent on the information being available in the systems, reporting software, and other records for detailed and root-cause analysis. For example, you could start by identifying the types of waste and providing percentages relating to the types identified, thus allowing management to address priorities quickly.

Lean Six Sigma

"Lean Six Sigma combines Lean Manufacturing and Six Sigma to improve operational efficiency and performance by eliminating defects, over-production, waiting, non-utilised talent, transportation, inventory, motion, and extra-processing or excessive processing." (*Source: Aris.com*)

Total Quality Management (TQM)

Total Quality Management (TQM) experienced worldwide success in the 1980s and early 1990s. In the mid-1990s, other operational efficiency methodologies such as ISO 9000, Six Sigma, and Lean Six Sigma overtook TQM and began to be applied at a global scale and became industry-standard recognisable brands.

TQM standards include the following:

- The benchmark of quality is provided by customer requirements, therefore deciding the product's level of value. The requirements must be focused on the customers who define the quality. If customer needs have been addressed, the project is a success, and it's a failure if customer needs have not been addressed.

TQM Diagram

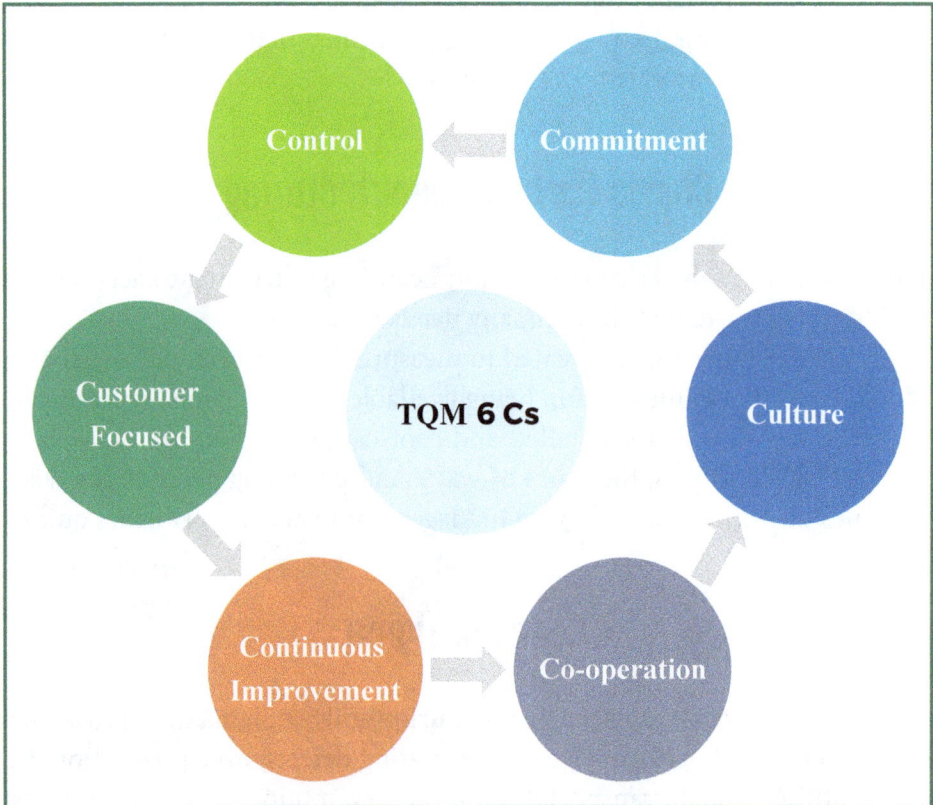

Figure 60: *TQM Principles*

- Executive management is responsible for quality improvement within the business, and their involvement, support and providing funding are critical to the project delivery being successful.
- Communication is critical, and businesses must have established communication channels that focus on the overall company objectives. The communication engagement will define who needs to be updated on progress throughout the TQM life cycle project from strategy to operational levels.

- The improvement for quality should be achieved in collaboration and alignment with system efficiencies. The system metrics can be obtained from system defect logs and customer complaints in relation to system performance.
- Quality improvement must be a continuous process performed across the organisation. The main goal of documenting and following the processes is for quality management. If processes are documented, they need to be followed, otherwise, defects can arise, resulting in high costs for re-works and complaints.

Toyota Production System/Just-in-time

"Just-in-time (JIT) manufacturing, also known as just-in-time production or the Toyota Production System (TPS), originated in Japan, largely in the 1960s and 1970s and particularly at Toyota." (*Source: Toyota.com*)

"TPS is a process framework aimed at purchasing raw material based on customer orders and dispatching them to customers without holding stock or finished products." (*Source: Toyota.com*)

The benefits of JIT are as follows (*Source: Toyota.com*):

- Customer deliveries are made within the time frames requested, resulting in better customer relationships and zero delays.
- Reduction in labour costs by focusing production on orders that customers have made rather than holding inventory that customers haven't paid for.
- Reduction in inventory costs with zero inventory philosophy.
- Reduction in WIP stock costs.
- Space maximisation is facilitated by not having to hold any stock.
- Quality improvements by focusing on producing items that have been ordered, based on customer specifications.
- Increase production efficiency and cost savings.
- Reduction in the number of hours worked by employees on production lines.
- Increase production efficiencies and cost savings through reduced failures and defects by applying quality processes for checking with approval before despatch to the customer.

Overall, JIT frameworks can be successful, specifically where the company's supplier systems are integrated into their customers' systems.

Theory of Constraints

The theory of constraints (TOC) focuses on constraints that prohibit processes from being implemented successfully. There is always at least one constraint, and TOC uses a process to identify the constraint and restructure the organisation's rest around that constraint. (*Source: Leanproduction.com*).

A constraint is anything that prevents a requirement(s) or a goal from being achieved. The types of constraints are categorised in the following segments: equipment and systems, people, and business policies.

The four steps of identifying the constraints are as follows: (*Source: Leanproduction.com*)

- Identify the constraint.
- Decide how to eliminate the constraint.
- Subordinate and introduce the new requirement.
- Alleviate the condition and repeat the process.

Business Process Benchmarking with Competitors

This section focuses on comparing three competitors in an airline industry based on their main processes and industry benchmarks. The main goal is to show that airlines with robust quality processes tend to have better ratings than those whose quality processes are not that efficient in comparison with their competitors.

Efficiency is based on customers who rate the airline with feedback on their customer experience when interacting with the brand.

The industry-standard ratings play a critical role in influencing customers making decisions about which airline to use when travelling on short and long flights.

The benchmarking activity has taken three of the larger airlines in the world to compare the quality and outcome of their process based on the specific categories mentioned in the airline rating and overall customer satisfaction.

If quality standards have been followed and customers have been involved in designing those processes, customer experience and satisfaction are usually positive.

Airline Competitor Benchmarking

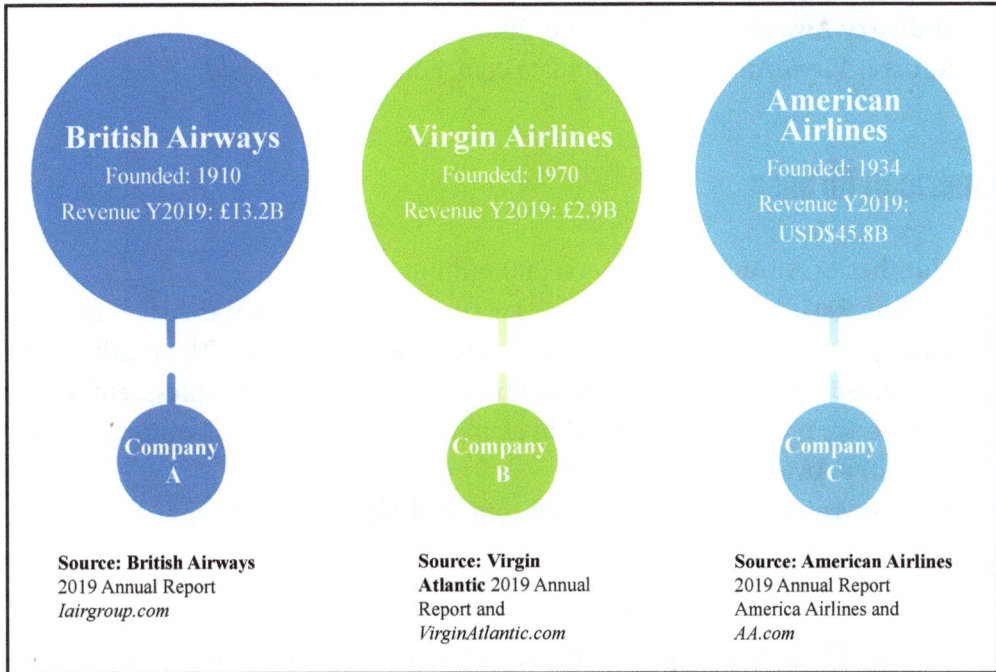

British Airways
Founded: 1910
Revenue Y2019: £13.2B

Virgin Airlines
Founded: 1970
Revenue Y2019: £2.9B

American Airlines
Founded: 1934
Revenue Y2019: USD$45.8B

Company A

Company B

Company C

Source: British Airways
2019 Annual Report
Iairgroup.com

Source: Virgin Atlantic 2019 Annual Report and *VirginAtlantic.com*

Source: American Airlines
2019 Annual Report
America Airlines and *AA.com*

Figure 61: *Benchmarking for Airline Competitors*

British Airways

Number of Annual Customers: 45 million (2019)
Airline Rating: "British Airways is certified as a four-star airline for the quality of its airports and onboard product and staff service. Product rating includes seats, amenities, food and beverages, IFE, cleanliness, etc., and the service rating is for both cabin staff and ground staff." (*Skyratings.com*)
Industry Awards: Business Traveller and multiple awards (2020)
Source: *BritishAirways.com* and *Skyratings.com*

Virgin Airlines

Number of Annual Customers: 5.7 million (2019) (*Statista.com*)
Airline Rating: "Virgin Atlantic is certified as a four-star airline for the quality of its airport and onboard product and staff service. The product rat-

ing includes seats, amenities, food and beverages, IFE, cleanliness, etc., and the service rating is for both cabin staff and ground staff." (*Skyratings.com*)
Industry Awards: Global Airline, 2021
Source: *VirginAtlantic.com, Statista.com*, and *Skyratings.com*

American Airlines

Number of Annual Customers: 200 million (2019)
Airline Rating: "American Airlines is certified as a three-star airline for the quality of its airport and onboard product and staff service. The product rating includes seats, amenities, food and beverages, IFE, cleanliness, etc., and the service rating is for both cabin staff and ground staff." (*Skyratings.com*)
Industry Awards: Not Available
Source: *AmericanAirlines.com/AA.com*, and *Skyratings.com*

How Operational Excellence Processes Contribute to Business Continuity

The Operational Excellence (OE) Strategy, including its objectives, must be driven by the corporate strategy.

The key benefits are as follows:

- Altered or improved management activities resulting from new systems, processes, business changes, and other types of renovations.
- Documentation of efficient processes and use of resources in the new business normal or contingency planning.
- Ensures cost reduction and provides efficient communication through relevant, engaged communication channels.
- Promotion of the required culture and training.
- Provides a beneficial partnership between suppliers on the value chain, ensuring that the business has the right capacity of resources to execute the required operational excellence and benchmarking with competitors.

Operational Excellence Strategy linked to Corporate Strategy

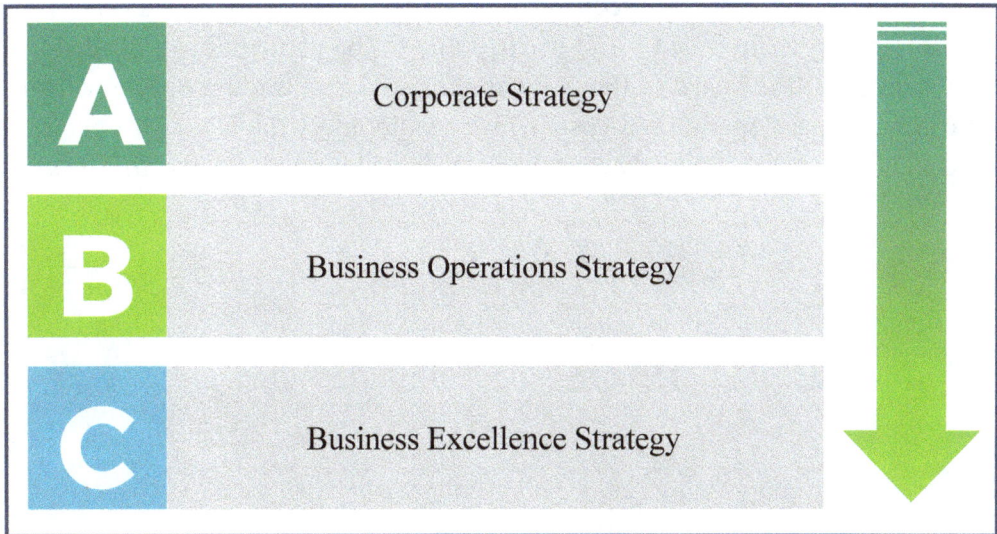

Figure 62: *Corporate Strategy Linked to Operational Excellence Strategy*

For a company to generate consistent revenue and continue trading, business operations need to be safeguarded against high-impact disruptions. COVID-19 affected all companies globally, but not all companies were affected in the same way. Some companies expanded their market share and generated significant profits. Amazon, for example, in 2020, generated $386B in revenue compared to $280B in 2019 with increased revenue by 73%. (*Source: Statista.com*).

For business operations to continue or recover from disruptions, the key areas needed must include robust business processes, advanced systems, assets, skilled human resources, and efficient business partners. (*Source: IBM.com*).

Also, during a global crisis, a business should be able to acquire new customers and retain existing customers consistently and predictably. The target here is a customer growth strategy supported by a robust operating model.

In the COVID era, remote work was mandatory; online retail shopping was the only option (in tandem with reduced offline shopping for groceries and other necessities). This meant that non-essential retailers had to transit to full capacity in the realm of online shopping. Otherwise, they would have potentially ceased to trade altogether without the online shopping channel.

This digital transition affected the companies differently – some were able to adapt to the new business landscape, while others couldn't.

Primark, one of the largest budget clothing retailers, chose specifically to sell its products offline only. The shopping channel preferred selling in high street stores to derive benefits from reduced costs associated with online trading.

"Revenues declined by £1.05B in 2020 due to the pandemic when all stores were closed but the board of the company insisted that trading online will significantly increase operational costs which would affect the low-cost operating model and prices subsequently charged to their customers." (*Source: BBC.com*)

Case Example

Process Improvement or Process Re-engineering Case Studies and Project Results [2021] Generated Extensive Cost Reduction and Improved Customer Satisfaction *(Sourced from Aimultiple.com, fifty-five process improvement case studies, and project results [2021])*

Business Name	Process Methodology	Process Software	Process Category	Process Benefits
Allianz Indonesia	Business Process Mapping (BPM)	Camunda	Legacy applications processes	· Process integration · Operational efficiencies
Deutsche Bahn Cargo	Business Process Mapping (BPM)	Camunda	Logistics	· Optimisation of European rail freight transport
Microsoft	Six Sigma		Operating Model	· Increased efficiency, accuracy, and service provided to customers
Npower	Robotic Process Automation (RPA)	Blue Prism		· $10M savings per year · 2 million hours of work automated per year
Siemens AG	Process Mining	Celonis	Service process management	· Automation of ordering channels · Standardisation of the process · Quick identification of inefficiencies
Starbucks	Lean Six Sigma	??	Customer services	· Reduced waiting times · Faster ordering processes
Telefonica 02	Robotic Process Automation (RPA)	Blue Prism	Fifteen processes representing 35% of back-office transactions	· Reduced need for FTE growth · Reduced turn-around time
Vodafone	Process Mining	Celonis	Payments	· Generated cost savings · Improved product lifecycles

Figure 63: *Successful Process Projects Across Multiple Sectors (Source: Research.Aimultiple.com)*

Summary

This chapter has covered the industry-standard process improvement methodologies, which include Six Sigma, lean fabricating, Lean Six Sigma, total quality management, the Toyota system production/just-in-time, and the theory of constraints from a high-level perspective.

The key lesson is to extract the principles from each framework and apply them accordingly to the projects that you are working on.

It's extremely important to always consider the deadlines on your project and effectively obtain the principles which will add maximum value to your projects.

Then, with regards to benchmarking, three airlines have been chosen to help show how process improvements are linked to customer satisfaction. Their star rating is based on processes such as the quality of the airport desk(s), onboard product and staff service, cleanliness, and service ratings for both cabin and ground staff.

These ratings are important because they are linked to customer experience and satisfaction based on the performance of each process.

The section on operational excellence explains how process improvement initiatives enable a company to achieve business continuity through process documentation and updates, process experts, and robust process software for management.

Lastly, the case example has provided company performance metrics in monetary terms to show how process methodologies and techniques such as business process mapping, Six Sigma, robotic process automation, Lean Six Sigma, and process mining frameworks have generated significant operational cost savings, revenue growth, service design and improvement in overall customer satisfaction.

Chapter Five

Customer Journey Mapping Techniques

Chapter Introduction

THIS CHAPTER LOOKS THROUGH a different lens, reviewing process mapping and focusing on customer journeys, sometimes known as customer processes. If a customer journey addresses customer requirements and their pain points, the customers are then likely to purchase from that retailer.

On the downside, if the customer journeys don't consider customer requirements, customers are likely to switch to alternative retailers.

Customer journeys are critical for any organisation because they are linked to profitability and market share. The rule is to always invest in customer journeys by optimising technology, process improvements, and designing products and services that customers are willing to purchase.

Chapter Learning Outcomes

In this chapter, you will learn the following topics:

- Definitions of customer journeys.
- Offline and online customer journey touchpoints.
- Customer journeys regarding product design.
- The design of customer journey processes.

- Business continuity for customer journeys.
- Customer journey benchmarks.

This chapter essentially addresses the importance of customer journey requirements which is at the centre of corporate strategies, technology, and operating model design to achieve profitability, customer growth, and customer satisfaction.

Customer Journeys Overviews

Have you ever thought about the impression your business makes on your customers online and offline (in physical stores)? You may be stunned by the contrasts between how employees see their business and how customers, including external stakeholders, perceive the same company.

Look at the feedback from the customer's side. If customers navigate the online store or contact your customer services, what do they experience? When customers purchase products, what aftercare support do they get? How would customers find support when they need their problems solved or have questions about your products and services that they have purchased?

Customer journey mapping is an outline of the processes, touchpoints, and emotions customers experience online and offline. This chapter focuses on defining customer journeys, mapping customer journey processes, and how customer journeys contribute to increasing sales for a company by designing a customer process that meets their needs.

Defining Customer Journeys

The customer journey is a method of diagrammatically showing the communications – or "touchpoints and emotions" – that a customer experiences when engaging with your business online or offline.

It starts from business strategy, pre-development, product design, customer feedback forums, artificial intelligence (AI) in data analytics, and post-development customer research, followed by the launch. The process helps to pinpoint issues and understand customer wants and needs in a better way.

In some instances, customer journey mapping is used interchangeably with customer experience mapping, but the terms, however, are entirely different.

Customer Online and Offline Touch Points

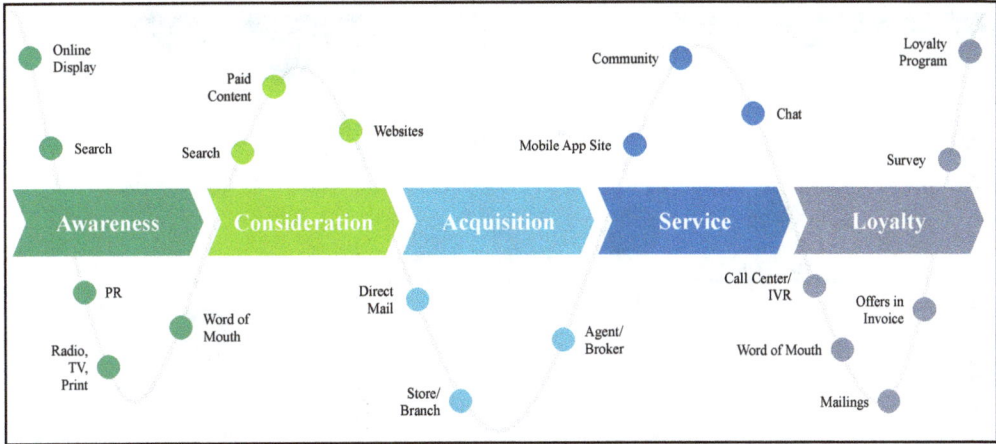

Figure 64: *Multi-Channel Touchpoints*

Revenue by Online Channel demonstrating the Success of Online Touch Points

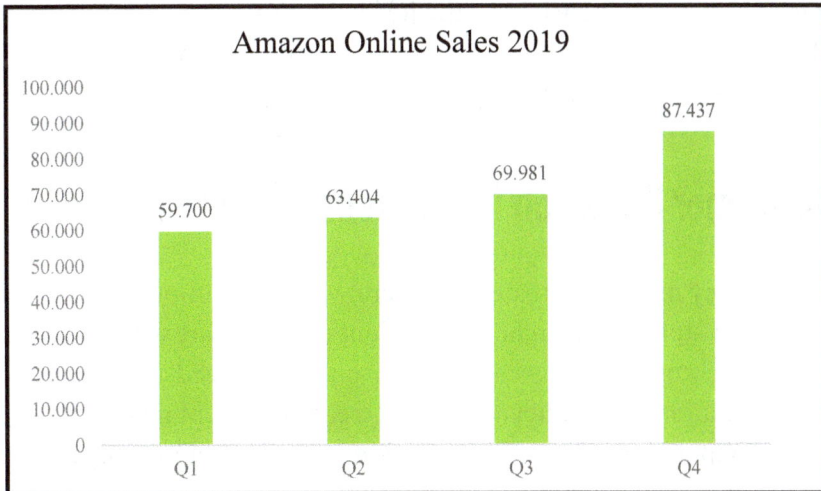

Figure 65: *Amazon Annual Report 2020*

Customer Offline Physical Store Touch Points

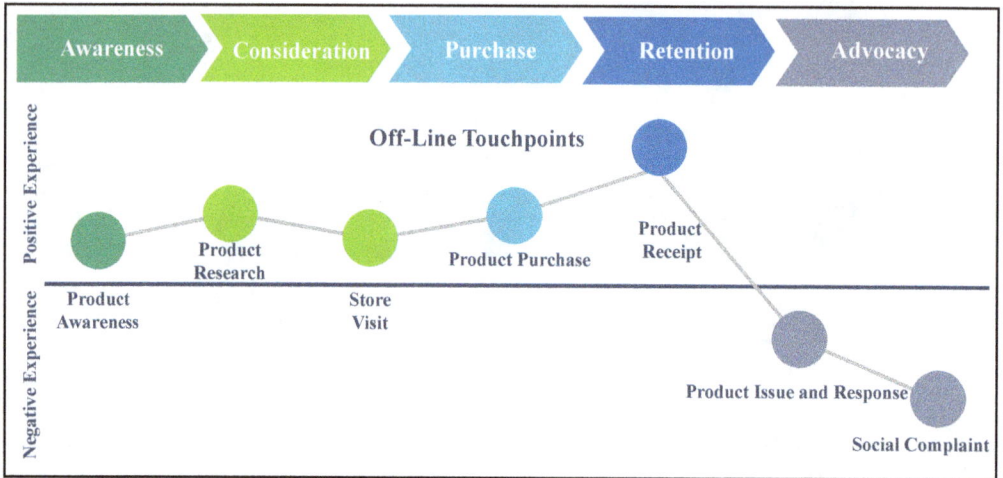

Figure 66: *Face-to-Face Touchpoints*

The customer journey is composed of the steps or processes the customer performs in purchasing and experiencing products and services. This includes the recording of emotions on the process. Customer experience covers, in much more detail, how well customer journeys have been designed to meet the needs and wants of customers focusing on the journey steps.

Customer experience is the metric to measure customer journey successes and failures based on the customer's perspective.

Customer Research for Product and Service Design

Customer journey maps are created in several ways. The important step involves the analysis of customer research. All excellent designs start with research.

The more a company knows about their customer needs, wants, and preferences, the more information they will use to create a concept map to meticulously research and help designers avoid assumptions and create a journey that customers will appreciate. The customer journey adds value to their corporate strategy and customer requirements.

Feedback surveys are considered direct ways of asking customers about their needs and what they require to meet these needs.

Similarly, interviewing customers is a great opportunity to ask many questions and even observe what they are not disclosing about their needs.

The customers will respond to a product in the framework of completing a specific task. Customer journey maps use storytelling and visualisation to improve customer experience/interaction with the product over time.

This helps the design team to identify actionable opportunities to improve the current customer journey.

Quantitative analytical data provide valuable insights into the product's users (*Source: Transformation: The Journey to Customer-Centricity, 2015*). It also includes the deployment of artificial intelligence (AI) to better understand customers' behaviour, current needs, preferences, and predictions.

Conducting comparative and competitive research also provides excellent value. The study is based on observing how customers engage with the existing solutions and products both online and offline. Mapping out the competitor's customer journey is more revealing and used as a benchmark for performance analysis and future scope.

The other step involves identifying the customer journey through the customer lens. Before a design team starts mapping a customer journey, one must define what the questions to be examined are going to be.

After synthesising the research, the design team can understand the timeline or scope of the experience. Companies must also remember that customers are not considering the company's experience in micro-interaction. Mapping out the customer journey across every channel helps the designers to optimise the journey to bring about the overall customer experience.

To solve a certain problem for the customer, the mapping exercise should go to great lengths to include feedback from customers, building a map which, at each touchpoint, gives the customers a chance to learn more about research and even have a holistic experience in mind (*Source: Transformation: The Journey to Customer-Centricity, 2015*).

In the last five years, most global corporations seem to have acquired AI start-ups with the specific goal of understanding accurately and predicting customer needs, their wants and the ever-changing customer demands.

The acquisition of AI start-ups is intended to support their digital strategy and improve their ability to predict customers' shopping behaviours and direct consumer strategies. Nike acquired AI platform Select in 2019, and other companies such as Facebook, Amazon, Microsoft, and Apple have also made numerous AI acquisitions in recent history. (*Source: Techcrunch.com*)

This explains how customer journey design is critical for company sales success. Customer feedback is also essential as input for co-creating the product with the customers. In the design phase, the customer's voice is needed for incorporating ideas and customer requirements in the final product.

Customer Journey and Product Design

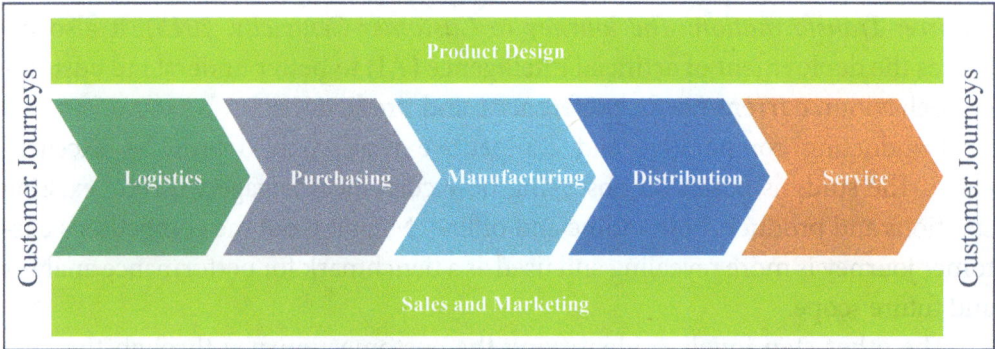

Figure 67: *Customer Research for Designing Customer Journeys*

Customer User Research

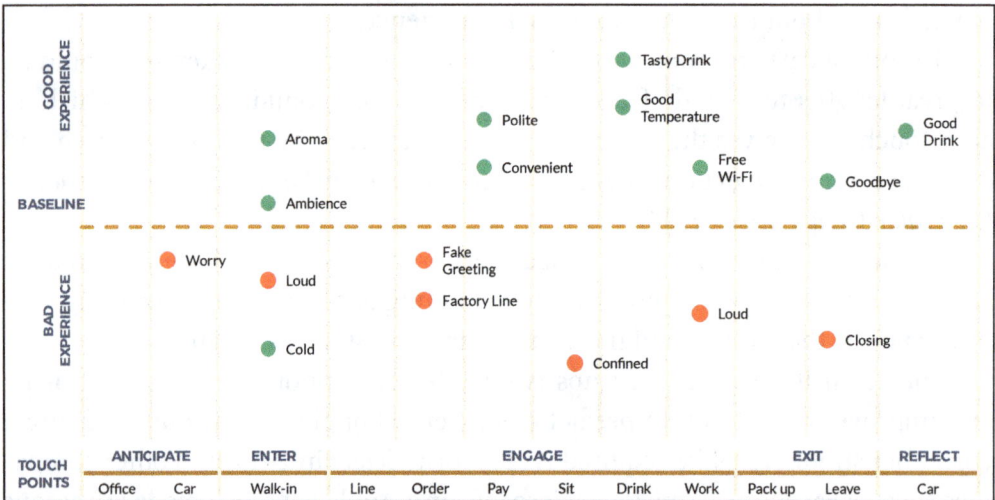

Figure 68: *Customer Research Feedback*

How to Design Customer Journey Processes

To document customer journeys for your business, consider the following steps:

Define Objectives

A great starting point is to define the objectives expected to be achieved from the customer journeys. This will enable the business to decide the scope of touchpoints that need to be mapped and documented for online and/or offline channels.

Let's review one excellent example to show how the customer journey objective could be used to improve customer experience metrics by improving company-wide customer service processes. To achieve this goal, the business would need to document the whole customer journey end-to-end and ensure that the customer journey objectives are accomplished on the specific shopping channels.

Perform Data Analysis

Identify the reasons customers engage with the business. What are customers obtaining from the website? How do customers navigate the website? Study their steps and time spent on the website. Ensure you get clear data analytics about the customer and their behaviour when interacting with the interfaces.

When customers purchase a product or service from your business, they either have a positive or negative experience. Feedback about these customer experiences can be used to create personas for your customers, and the information will provide input in designing the customer journey.

The research can be obtained from third parties, AI data analytics, feedback from customer services, marketing, and other internal functions that engage and collaborate with customers directly or indirectly across the business.

This enables the business to obtain a deeper understanding of the shopping channels that the customers use to engage with your company and the level of service they are provided when using those channels.

Identify Customer Touchpoints

Customers interact with your company using a variety of "touchpoints." These may include in-store activity, phone calls, online navigation, sales and marketing campaigns, purchase, social media, and other touchpoints.

When business touchpoints have been identified, what service is being provided to the customer, and which stakeholders are customer-facing? Where would the customers be able to find support information? Is it easy for customers to obtain your customer services contact details if they have questions?

Is the company providing accurate information that helps customers on specific touchpoints, or does the company provide misleading and inaccurate information? This could involve sales and/or marketing teams providing communications that are frustrating to customers. Based on the information gathered, it's important to identify the touchpoints and document the sequence of interactions the customer has with your organisation.

Map Customer Journey

There are many different diagrams that can be used to document a customer journey map. One great technique is the employment of cross-functional swim lanes.

The first step is to identify the triggers, and the sequence of steps until the end, followed by creating swim lanes that depict the customer flows and highlighting the problem points that depict areas requiring process improvement.

The touchpoints with customers, the emotions and feelings they experience on the customer journey can be used to determine the functions that are causing problems and where change is required at the business operational level.

Analyse the Current State Customer Journey

You will have to validate the current state customer journey by engaging with the right functions before designing the future state customer journey. You can do this by requesting input from a focus group, third parties, client discussions, and/or different internal departments in your organisation.

The current state analysis will enable the business functions to measure their customer journey's effectiveness by identifying the weaknesses, strengths, opportunities, and threats based on the customer journey metrics and KPIs.

To perform further analysis, refer to the customer journey maps/objectives, and determine the opportunities that can be optimised.

Listed below are some common issues that may help with the analysis:

- Does the business provide the customer with excess data/contacts or no information at all?
- Do customers have access to correct information and are the customer services easily available to access?
- Are the customer touchpoints efficiently implemented in how they flow or are designed to meet customer needs?
- Does the company have specific functions responsible for customer services so that they're not confusing to customers? Or does the company have multiple departments and functions performing this activity, causing customer frustration and poor service quality?

Current State Customer Journey Website Channel

Customer Journey Shopping On Website Channel		
Customer Actions		
Browse on Website	Choose Products	Login/ Register New Account
Touch Points		
Landing Page	Product Pages	Payment Page
Any Web Page	Cart Page	Order Page
Retailer Operational Systems		
Receive Customer Details to Update Marketing Systems	Receive Data to Update Inventory and Stock Systems After 24 Hours	Send Payment Details to Finance and CRM Systems After 5 Hours
		Send Order to Logistics and CRM Systems After 10 Hours
Customer Emotions		
☹	☹	☹
Pain Points		
Landing Page Takes Too Long to Load	Stock and Inventory System Updates Not Real Time	Order Confirmations Take 24 Hours to be Sent to Customer
Possible Solutions		
Improve Landing Page and Website Loading and Speed Navigation	Provide Real Time Stock and Inventory Updates on Website	Send Customer Order Confirmation Within 5 Minutes of Making Payment

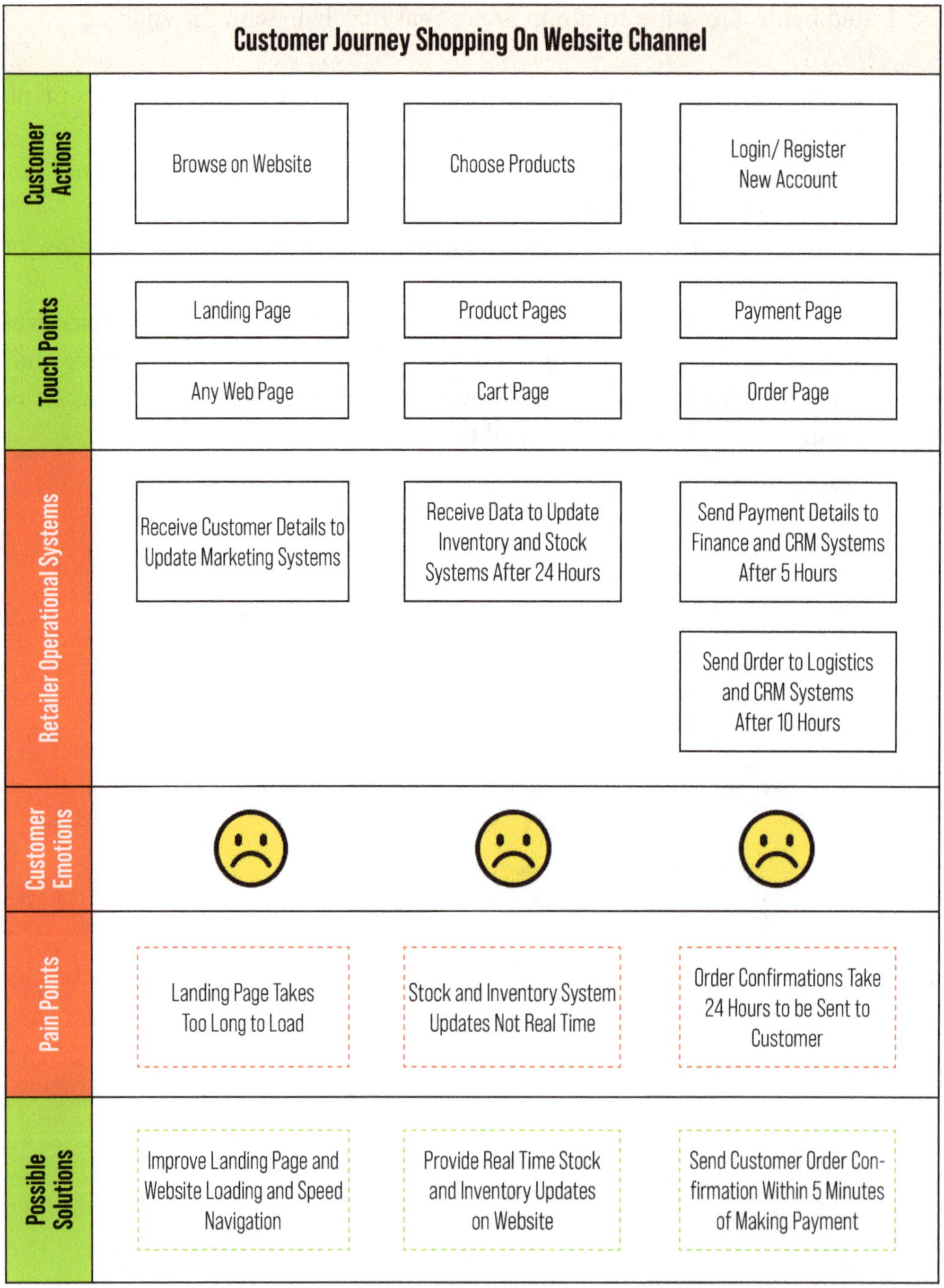

Figure 69: *Current State Customer Journey Website Channel*

Continuous Improvement and Future State Customer Journey

Defining Future State Customer Journey Website Channel

Customer Journey Shopping On Website Channel		
Customer Actions		
Browse on Website	Choose Products	Login/ Register New Account
Touch Points		
Landing Page	Product Pages	Payment Page
Any Web Page	Cart Page	Order Page
Retailer Operational Systems		
Marketing Systems Receive Customer Details Real Time	Receive Data to Update Inventory and Stock Systems Real Time	Send Payment Details to Finance and CRM Systems Real Time
		Send Order to Logistics and CRM Systems Real Time
Customer Emotions		
🙂	🙂	🙂
Solutions Implemented		
Improved Landing Page and Website Loading and Speed Navigation	Real Time Stock and Inventory Updates on Website	Customer Order Confirmation Sent Within 5 Minutes of Making Payment

Figure 70: *Future State Customer Journey Requirements*

For continuous improvement, it is important to ensure that the customer journey maps are updated with accurate information about the touchpoints so that they can help understand the root cause of the issues.

Updating customer journeys ensures that customer needs are taken into consideration and relevant information for that transformation is provided.

The business will be able to capture the new ways that the organisation interacts with customers for improving and providing better customer service.

Updating customer journeys is a costly activity that requires the sales and marketing strategy to include funding for resources that will be responsible for the customer journey tasks and continuous improvement.

If funding or resources are not allocated for updating the customer journeys, the information will be out of date and not useful for the current business operations.

Customer Journeys Post-COVID-19 Crisis

Meeting customer expectations must be the highest priority for any ongoing business. Business continuity ensures that retailers can achieve this objective, whether in a crisis due to unexpected events or in the "normal" operating model.

Due to COVID-19, there have been significant volume shifts across global shopping channels, both on and offline. The website is now the primary customer touchpoint for both essential and non-essential retailers.

This shift has resulted in high customer service requests, inbound calls, business process changes, and technology transforming the business operating models.

The company supply chain has had to be robust to ensure business continuity for delivering products and services within time frames that meet customer needs.

Consistent customer service between on-shore and off-shore resource needs has to be prioritised to ensure quality service for customers.

If the products and services being provided fail to meet customer needs or expectations, revenue loss is expected, and the company's future in terms of its 'going concern' status may be brought into question.

Customer Journeys Pre-Covid-19 Crisis

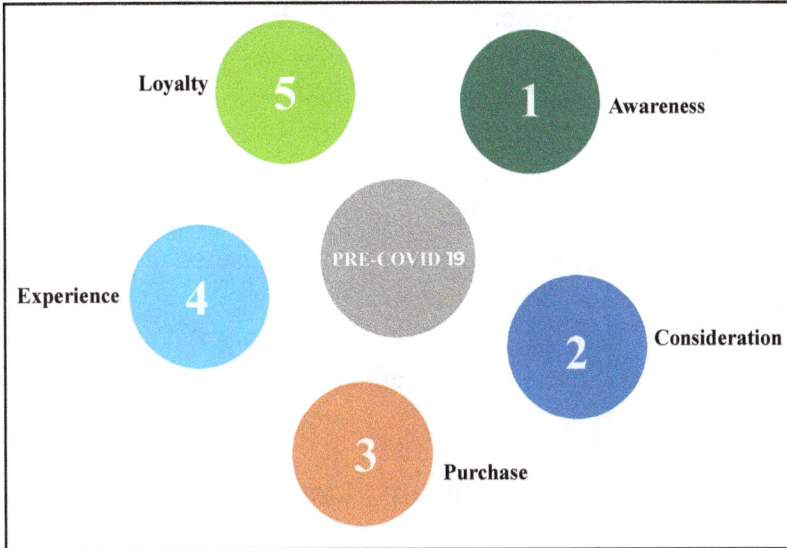

Figure 71: *Customer Journeys Pre-COVID 19 (Source: Oddballmarketing.com)*

Customer Journeys Post-Covid-19 Crisis

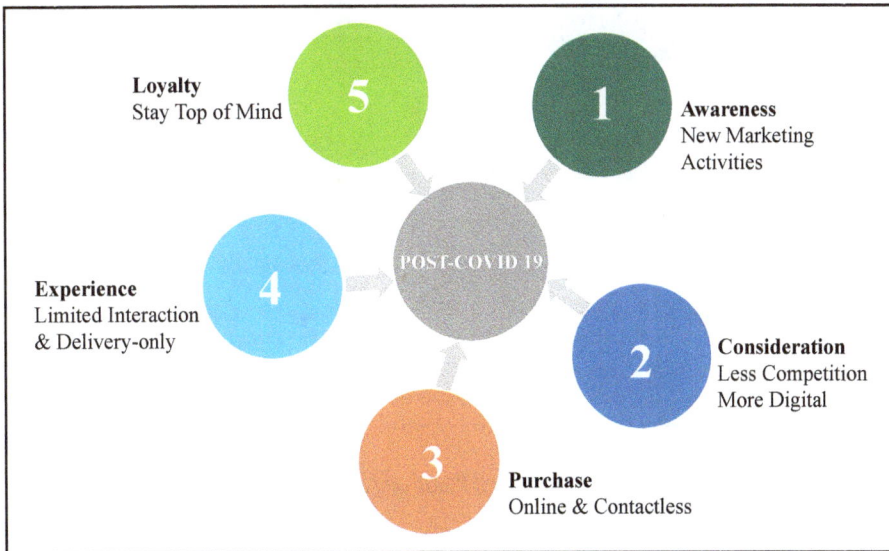

Figure 72: *Customer Journeys Post-COVID-19 (Source: Oddballmarketing.com)*

Customer Journey Process Benchmarking for Competitors

The benchmarking in this section is for Amazon and eBay, which are well-recognised global brands in online retail. The process categories address the number of customers each of the sites has and the annual revenue generated determining growth or decline.

The increase in annual customers indicates growth while a decline signifies that the company is having its market share reduced with other companies taking over its market space. The online retail sector for business-to-business and customer-to-business models is excessively competitive.

Other companies competing in this sector are Etsy, Rakuten, Bonanza, eBid, Alibaba, Ruby Lane, and many other retailers.

Customer Journey Benchmarking with Competitors

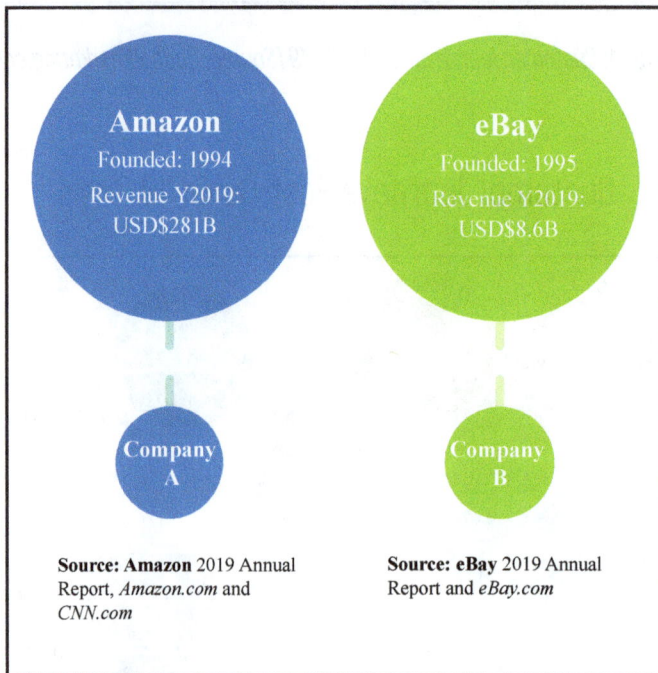

Amazon
Founded: 1994
Revenue Y2019:
USD$281B

eBay
Founded: 1995
Revenue Y2019:
USD$8.6B

Company A

Company B

Source: Amazon 2019 Annual Report, *Amazon.com* and *CNN.com*

Source: eBay 2019 Annual Report and *eBay.com*

Figure 73: *Online and Retail and Benchmarking*

Amazon

Channel: Online store
Number of Retail Customers: Approx. 200 million Prime accounts in 2020 and 150 million Prime Accounts in 2019 (*Statista.com*)
Success Criteria: eCommerce online and mobile retail
Business Record: Amazon 2020 revenue exceeded $386 billion and net profits increased by 84% mainly due to the COVID-19 pandemic which contributed to the organisation becoming the main global online retailer.
Growing or Declining: Growing
Source: *Amazon.com, Statista.com, CNN.com*

eBay

Channel: Online store
Number of Retail Customers: 185 million (2020) (*Statista.com*)
Success Criteria: "eBay's success is attributed to its unique business plan: allowing individuals or businesses to list new or used items for auction for a meagre fee." (*Forbes.com*)
Business Record: Revenue of $8.6 billion in 2019 and $10.2 billion in 2020 (*Statista.com*)
Growing or Declining: Growing
Source: *eBay.com, Statista.com, Forbes.com*

How the Customer Journey Processes Contribute to Business Continuity

Customer Journeys contribute to business continuity by aligning with the corporate strategy and integrating all departments within the organisation.

The goal is to understand how the processes in each function add value to maintaining and changing the customer journeys.

Due to COVID-19, more companies than ever before are investing in customer journeys to better understand their critical business operating model.

Every touchpoint on the customer journey either creates a positive or negative customer experience. Therefore, it's important to define roles and responsibilities of the departments and determine where the resources need to be invested to help with contributing to improving customer journeys for the organisation.

The other goal is to understand the pain points on the customer journey to define the change required for meeting customer needs.

Customer Journey Alignment to Corporate Strategy

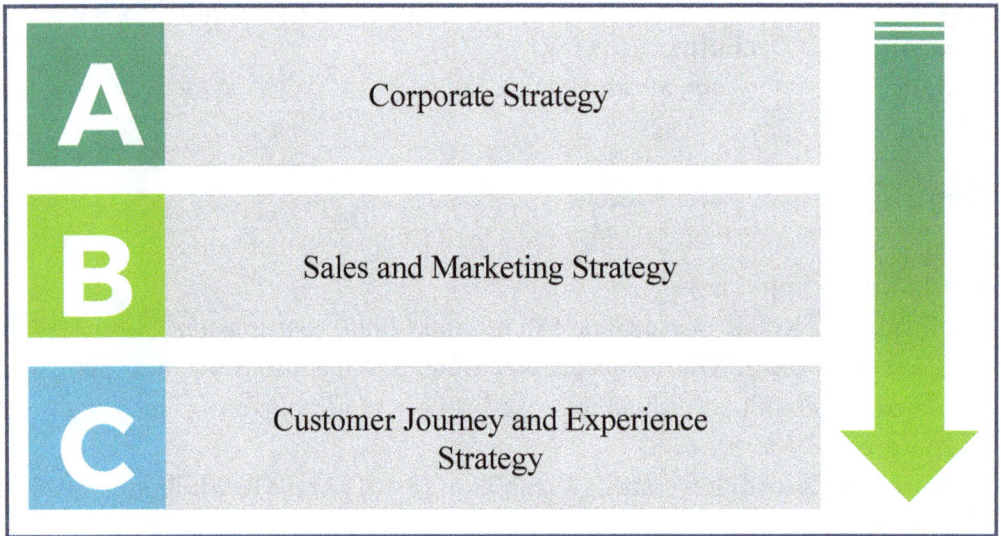

Figure 74: *Customer Journey Strategy*

For a business to sustain profitability, it is necessary to invest in product design, and deliver products and services which create positive experiences on the customer journeys, both online and offline.

The organisational structure plays a key role in ensuring that each function performing critical activities on the customer journey is provided with updated documented business processes, business procedures, training, relevant system access, and data management techniques to prevent loss of data.

The culture of the employees is also vital to make sure they support process improvement and customer-centricity and align with business policies in executing their respective tasks. Human resources will need to define the skills and behaviour which support the corporate strategy, tactics, and operations.

Case Example

The rise and fall of Blockbuster and how it's surviving with just one store left (*Sourced from Business Insider, 2020*)

Blockbuster dominated the video industry in the late 1990s and owned over 9,000 video rental stores in the USA, employing 84,000 people worldwide with 65 million registered customers and earned $800 million of late fees alone.

In 2010, Blockbuster filed for bankruptcy with almost $1 billion in debt because the company failed to compete with Netflix and other players for DVD mail services and failed to invest in digital technology.

Critical factors that led to Blockbuster's decline

- Executive leadership refused to invest in digital technology with their corporate strategy centred on face-to-face physical channels.
- No investment for building technology innovations because the company was extensively focused on the physical store experience rather than considering the emerging digital channels on the customer journeys and customer experience.
- Competitor Netflix created the DVD-by-mail rental service which offered customers a better service experience because all customers had to do was mail the DVDs rather than having the inconvenience of going to the store and paying late fees when they were late returning the DVDs.
- Blockbuster competitors optimised technology and the internet for improving customer journeys and experience through digital video rental channels.
- Blockbuster had the opportunity to acquire Netflix, but their executive team was too laser-focused on the dimensional shopping experience and disregarded the alternative channels which signalled the future.
- The Netflix DVD competitor offers were more attractive, giving customers better customer experiences, such as the following:
  - Online facility to order DVDs which meant that customers had the luxury to order DVDs at any time they wanted without having to be

constrained by the store opening times. Also, this feature allowed customers the opportunity to see all the catalogue of movies available in the comfort of their homes or wherever they had access to the internet.

– Customers could order three movies at a time at a much lesser price than Blockbuster rental charges.

– Not imposing late fees for video rentals that allowed the customers to keep the DVDs for as long as they wanted.

– Next day or one-day delivery after placing order.

– Provided prepaid envelopes for customers to send back and order new movies when they wanted to place new orders.

– Rental charges were $20 a month with no late fees applied.

Blockbuster's delay in entering the competition was obvious since they introduced the online DVD mail services five years after Netflix had launched and dominated the industry. At that point, Blockbuster had lost a significant market share with Netflix generating revenues of $116 in 2009.

Key Lessons

Every corporate strategy must prioritise technology, digital technology, customer journeys, customer experience, business processes, and customer offerings if the company wants to sustain incredible success for the long term.

If the company does not invest in customer journeys and technology, then unfortunately, it will decline and cease to exist like Blockbuster.

Every business strategy must evaluate how the processes in each function add value, and, if they are not adding value, then they must stop investing in those processes and activities.

Summary

This chapter has defined the concept of customer journeys as the process that customers experience when interacting with the company's brand.

Explanation of the steps involved in designing a customer journey (e.g., defining the objectives, continuous improvements, and defining the customer touchpoints):

- Customer journeys are important because the process that customers go through defines the customer experience and customer satisfaction.
- If customer needs are met, and the journeys in terms of digital or offline experience achieve expectations, revenue and profits will be high because customers will keep coming back.
- If, on the other hand, customer needs are not particularly in relation to the customer journeys, revenues will decline, and customers are likely to switch to retailers that offer them better products they are looking for, better offers and a better customer journey they will be happy with.
- In that situation, the company will lose customers and have a reduced market share. Having consistent customer growth through retention and acquisition must be the priority of all businesses in sustaining performance, both in the short term and long term.

It's fascinating to learn that the majority of companies had not prioritised customer journeys and customer experience measurements before the COVID-19 crisis. The effects of the pandemic have forced businesses to invest in customer journeys. Overall, designing customer journeys that meet customer needs is critical for any company to succeed in outperforming their competitors, retaining existing clients, and attracting new customers in all product portfolios and business segments.

Chapter Six

Redefining the Customer Experience

Chapter Introduction

THIS CHAPTER IS LINKED to chapter five, which focuses on customer journeys. Customer experience is about measuring customer journeys to determine customer satisfaction and dissatisfaction. Customer relationship management (CRM) systems are used specifically for this purpose.

Process metrics are a great approach for understanding customer experience and the root cause of issues impacting customer needs not being addressed.

The key customer experience measurements in organisations will usually start with the volume of sales in connection with new and existing customers.

Chapter Learning Outcomes

As you read this chapter, you will learn the following:

- Definitions of customer experience.
- Customer experience measurement metrics.
- How to link customer experiences with customer journeys.
- Financial benefits of the customer experience.
- Benchmarking examples of the customer experience.

Process improvement models such as Six Sigma are a great way for coming up with suitable solutions to address a company's customer experience. If metrics are high for the two measurements, it's usually a good indication, but if the two metrics are in decline, it usually means that customers are dissatisfied.

Customer Experience and Connection with Customer Journeys

Customer experience relates to how customers interact with the business, either directly or indirectly. Direct contact mostly takes place while purchasing items and using products and services, with the customer often starting the process.

Indirect contact involves unplanned encounters with representations of the products, services, or brands of that company. In most cases, customer experience is in the form of word-of-mouth recommendations or advertising, criticisms, reviews, news reports, social media reports, and industry rankings.

These encounters could also take place through emails (*Source: Transformation: The Journey to Customer-Centricity, 2015*). For a brand to be successful, it must shape the customer experiences by embedding the fundamental value proposition in offering each feature. The scope of service quality matters the most when it comes to customer experience, and it helps to ensure that the products are delivered on time and that customers can easily track their parcels.

It's also important to highlight that customer experience can be mainly reflected by the different types of a company's offerings based on product design and customer service quality. This extends to the company's product packaging, advertising, and communications about the maximum number of features of its products and services. The focus is on measuring the customer journey performance through the following metrics: new customers acquired, existing customers retained, customers who left but returned, and customers who are leaving. This measurement includes customer satisfaction metrics such as net promoter scoring (NPS), customer satisfaction score (CSAT), customer service satisfaction (CSS), customer reviews, customer complaints, and many others.

Customer Experience Success Demonstrated by Online Revenue

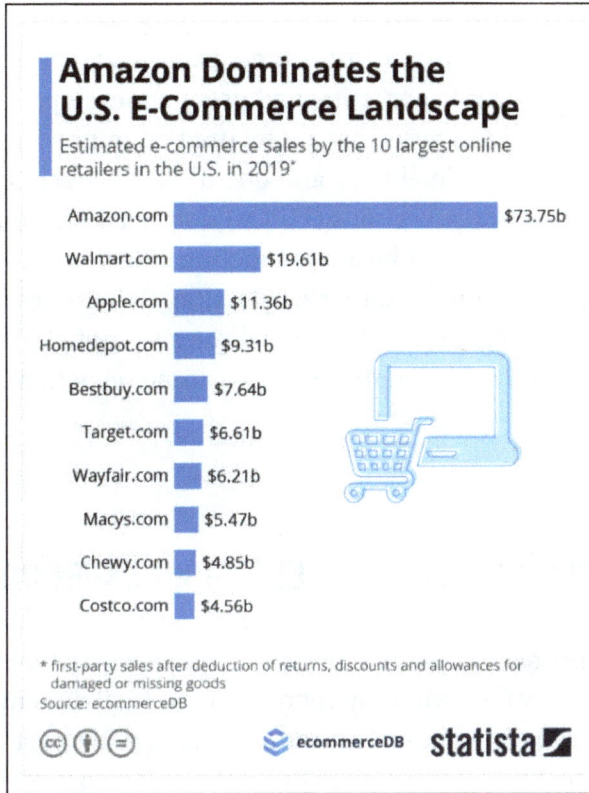

Amazon Dominates the U.S. E-Commerce Landscape

Estimated e-commerce sales by the 10 largest online retailers in the U.S. in 2019*

Retailer	Sales
Amazon.com	$73.75b
Walmart.com	$19.61b
Apple.com	$11.36b
Homedepot.com	$9.31b
Bestbuy.com	$7.64b
Target.com	$6.61b
Wayfair.com	$6.21b
Macys.com	$5.47b
Chewy.com	$4.85b
Costco.com	$4.56b

* first-party sales after deduction of returns, discounts and allowances for damaged or missing goods
Source: ecommerceDB

ecommerceDB   statista

Figure 75: *Amazon Dominates US E-Market (Source: Statista.com)*

Amazon and Walmart dominate the e-commerce landscape because their customer journey processes are contributing to positive customer experience. This goes to show that customer experience as a measure can be a great indicator to help businesses allocate resources to achieve customer satisfaction.

Through customer experience data analytics and customer journey analysis, companies can identify business functions contributing to positive customer experience and those not adding value to customer satisfaction.

The company must efficiently use the customer information it acquires internally from sales and other departments, including external data sources, to understand customer preferences and even their reliability. (*Source: Customer Experience Strategy: Building a Customer Experience Organisation", 2015 publication*).

To achieve an optimised customer experience, the business needs to have efficient integrated CRM systems for recording and measuring the customer experience.

Each function must contribute to customer experience even though they have specialist roles. For example, marketing and product development have different roles, but they both perform tasks that are focused on improving customer experience to increase revenue, timeliness, and quality, and reduce costs.

As high performing organisations (HPOs) dominate e-commerce retail, it is important to mention that their business functions must be well-integrated with a common goal of improving customer satisfaction. Otherwise, customer experience will be impacted negatively if functional roles are not clearly defined across the organisation and how they contribute to customer experience.

Financial Benefits of Customer Experience

- Firstly, it ensures that there is a higher customer lifetime value. The customer lifetime value primarily represents the total amount of money that a customer spends on business products and services over a certain period. Understanding this number gives the brand a chance to identify the amount they can invest in retaining customers and getting new ones.
- The real benefit of the customer experience is to ensure that the number of customers increases in the business. On the other hand, repeated customers represent a stronger customer loyalty to a brand (*Source: Walden, 2017*).
- It also looks at the quality of a firm's products and is influenced by several interactions that a person has with a firm. Most companies introduce reward programs to communicate and collect customer data and these strategies tend to increase customer conversions also.
- Walden (2017) claims that customer experience also reduces customer churn. Businesses tend to see a rise in customer lifetime value, and they benefit from customer turnover and reduced churn. It becomes more costly to get new customers, retain them, and expend resources to ensure that they are happy and do not experience longer engagements. Customer experiences are improved through regular touchpoints that include frequent phone calls, email updates, and even customer appreciation events.

- This ensures that a brand stays in the customers' minds. The customer experience also increases the equity of the brand. Brand equity is described as the value of a brand in the consumers' eyes. Brand equity has a lot to do with the emotions that a consumer has when thinking of a brand. The company must deliver on the promises of providing high-quality products and be responsive to the customers. A company with positive brand equity has many fans, and the customers are happy with the products. They post positive reviews about the brand on social media to communicate their customer satisfaction.

- According to *Transformation: The Journey to Customer-Centricity* (2015), customer experience also facilitates high customer retention. Brands have higher brand equity and keep their customers. Excellent customer experience shows that the companies are fast in resolving issues, staying in touch with the customers, and rewarding loyal customers. The company also appreciates its customers; that, in turn, strengthens its positive perception. Higher customer retention increases the number of sales, and it is an easier way to increase the ROI from the initial sales conversion.

Customer Experience Process Benchmarking with Competitors

The benchmarking of customer experience with Nike and Adidas, two of the world's largest sportswear companies, is detailed below.

Customer experience is significantly improved through investments to understand customer needs and deliver that experience through customer journey mapping and processes that employ innovative marketing strategies to reach targeted audiences.

Both organisations have acquired AI start-ups with the goal of understanding and predicting customer needs, and then delivering what customers want.

Nike and Adidas Revenue Benchmarking

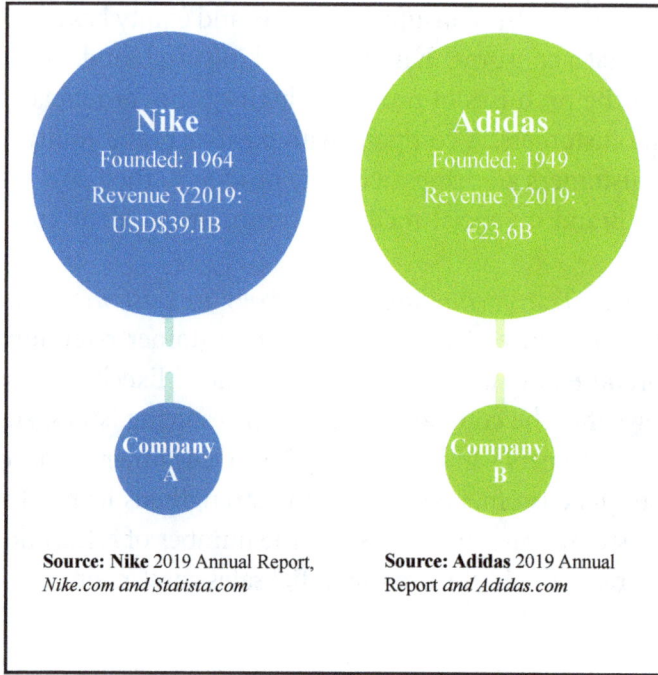

Nike
Founded: 1964
Revenue Y2019:
USD$39.1B

Adidas
Founded: 1949
Revenue Y2019:
€23.6B

Company
A

Company
B

Source: Nike 2019 Annual Report, *Nike.com and Statista.com*

Source: Adidas 2019 Annual Report *and Adidas.com*

Figure 76: *Customer Experience Benchmarks*

Nike

Market-share: Industry leader with $39.1 billion in revenues in 2019
Investments in Customer Experience: Acquired AI Start-Up Select and TraceMe in 2019 to expand their customer and digital strategy for contributing to customer predictive analytics. "Nike, Inc. acquired TraceMe to supplement the company's content strategy on Nike-owned platforms." (*Techcrunch.com*)
Marketing Budgets: $3.5 billion (*Statista.com*)
Industry Awards: Footwear Shoe Awards, 2020 (*Footwearnews.com*)
Source: *Nike.com, Techcrunch.com, Footwearnews.com*

Adidas

Market-share: Second largest athletic retailer with €23.6 billion in 2019
Investments in Customer Experience: AI Salesforce CRM Systems, business process improvement through operating one system, visible business pro-

cesses to enable customer-facing teams, and a centralized advanced system for customer analytics and customer experience transformation (*Salesforce.com*)
Marketing Budgets: €3 billion in 2019 (*Statista.com*)
Industry Awards: Innovative brand of the year 2020 (Sports Industry Awards 2020)
Source: *Adidas.com, Salesforce.com, Statista.com, Sportindustryawards.com*

How Customer Experience Processes Contribute to Business Continuity

The marketing strategy's goal is to attract and retain customers and be linked to the corporate strategy. Customer experience processes are dependent on the marketing strategy being linked to the corporate strategy.

Customer Experience Strategy

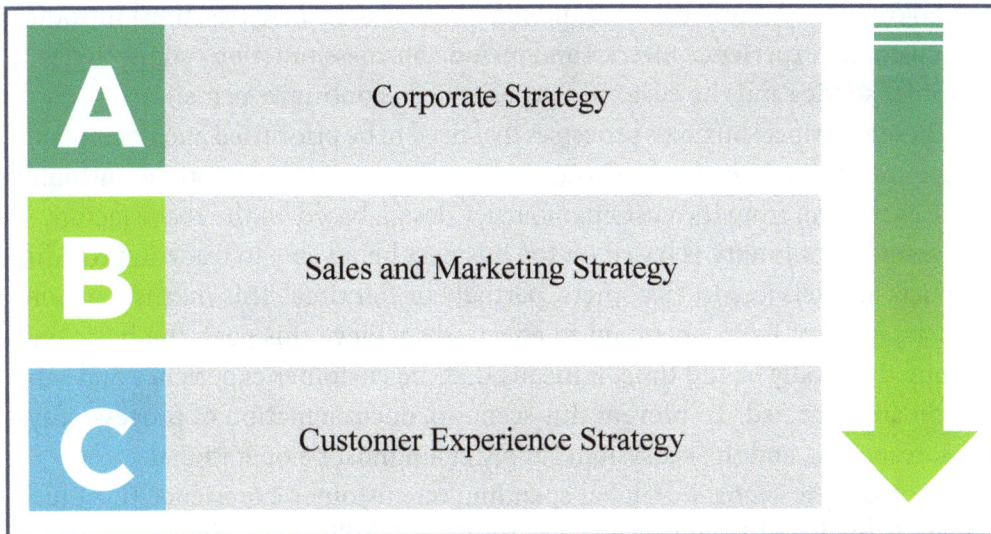

Figure 77: *Customer Experience Strategy linked to Corporate Strategy*

The marketing strategy asks the following questions *(Source: strategy.pwc.com)*:

- Who is the chosen customer? This requires customer journey and customer experience analytics to understand the pain points and wants.
- What does the customer need, and how does the business satisfy the customer's needs? What is the value proposition? What can we offer to the customer?
- Does the business understand customer needs at a granular level? How is the business going to attract such customers? Who are the competitors? How does the business exceed its performance and increase market share?
- How is the enterprise going to engage and get them interested in their products and services? How will they reach their customers, and which are the preferred shopping channels, online and or offline? How does the customer leverage their ecosystem of suppliers and partners?
- How does the business maximise its operating model capabilities using systems, processes, talented people, and others to meet customer needs?
- What is the CRM solution to address customer needs and analysis?

Customer satisfaction is dependent on CRM technology improvements defined as part of business enterprise architecture embedded in the business operating model. The business operating model components, like business processes, CRM technology, innovation business functions, and AI data analytics, must introduce new customer experience metrics and include business functions connected with customer service and the customer experience in continuity plans.

These are critical business processes that need to be prioritised and documented for the transfer of knowledge. Customer experience and the emotions customers experience result from the customer journey design based on the above factors.

Business continuity is based on the business being able to trade in providing products and services to customers, partially or full time. This means that company assets must be in operation to effectively achieve this goal. If a business is disrupted partially or full time, it means that the customer experience and satisfaction are impacted. To prevent this scenario, documentation of processes, systems, resources, and the ecosystem supply chain must be operational.

According to *Statista*, "Global spending on customer experience (CX) technology is predicted to increase from around 500 billion U.S. dollars in 2019 to over 640 billion by 2022. Companies are investing in CX to increase their market share.

Thanks to the growing popularity of internet-connected consumer electronic devices, companies have more information on consumer experiences and needs than ever before. Simple consumer demographic information can now be expanded to include extremely detailed usage and preference information, providing companies with the ability to precisely analyse their consumers' experience and satisfaction. CX products provide companies with these analysis tools which help to influence business strategy based on the results." (*Statista.com*)

Customer Experience (CX) Post-COVID 19 Crisis

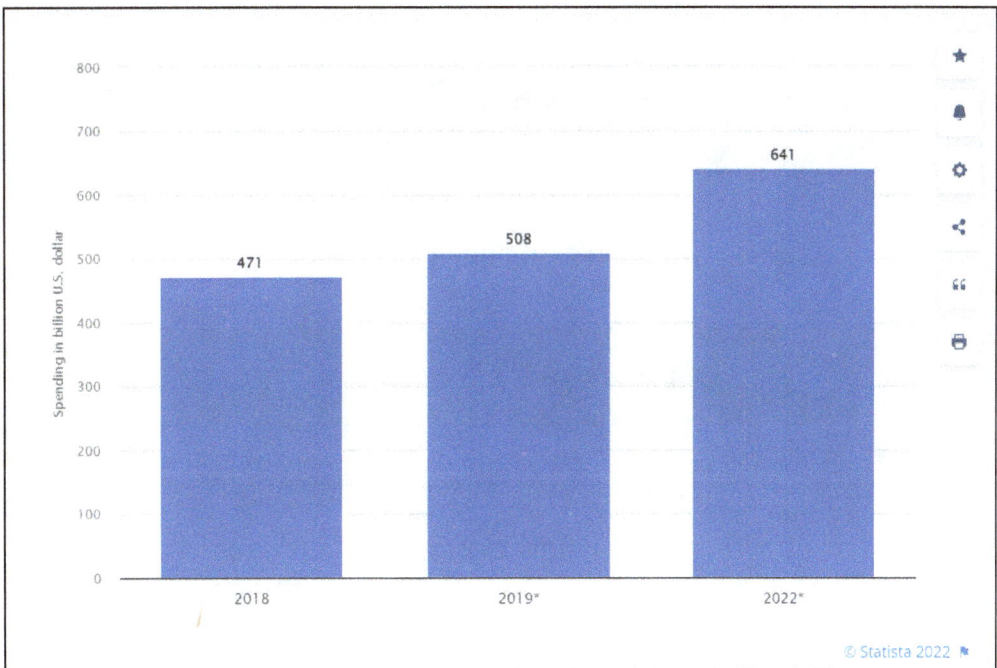

Figure 78: *CX Technology Spending 2018 to 2022 (Source: Statista.com)*

Case Example

Amazon's Customer Relationship Management (CRM) Strategy (*Source: Expertmarket.co.uk*)

Amazon is growing significantly at a rapid rate every single year. In Q3 2020, the company reports showed net sales of $96.15 billion, a 37.4% increase from the same period in 2019. So how *did* Amazon transform itself from a small online bookseller to a global online digital dominance?

Here are some reasons, provided at a high-level, showing how the online retailer started trading as an online bookseller to become one of the world's largest companies.

Amazon's Business Timeline

Amazon's Business Since Inception
1994: Jeff Bezos founds company as an online bookseller.
1997: Reaches one million customer accounts.
1998: Expands into selling CDs and DVDs.
2001: Makes first profit in the final quarter of the year.
2005: Launches Amazon Prime.
2007: Launches the Kindle e-reader.
2017: Acquires supermarket chain Whole Foods Market.
2020: In February, Amazon becomes just the fourth tech company in the world to reach a valuation of $1 trillion.
2021: Amazon purchases eleven aircraft from Delta Air Lines and West Jet Airlines to join Amazon Air marking the e-commerce titan's burgeoning entry into the cargo network space.

Figure 79: *Amazon History (Source: Expertmarket.co.uk)*

Reasons for Global Success

- CRM data capture for customers who shop online for creating a more relevant customised online experience.
- The interface is user-friendly, easy to use, and intuitive, alluring customers to shop online on the platform without any hassle.
- It lists various products that customers are looking for and are deliverable in most geographic regions globally.
- Tracking capability makes it easier for customers to see the locations of their parcels and when deliveries are expected.
- Same-day and next-day delivery services for urgent purchases that meet the growing expectations of the customers.
- Instant Return facility that earns customer loyalty to return to the site for other purchases over and over again.
- Hassle-free shopping experience once you create an account as a new customer, as is re-ordering purchases on the site as an existing customer.
- Offers and promotions customised to customers based on their shopping behaviour and preferences are important for marketing purposes.
- One-click online purchase makes the customer's complete shopping experience enjoyable, easy, and quick to complete.
- Use of Artificial Intelligence (AI) and robotics through AI start-up acquisitions such as Canvas Technology and many others enable understanding of customer needs.

Overall, Amazon is an HPO and a global retailer because of the strategic leadership teams, process management innovation, technology innovation, and other factors.

CRM is optimised extensively for customising customer needs, which is supplemented by a customer-centricity strategy, and AI/ robotics.

Summary

The goal of this chapter has been to define customer experience, which focuses on customer satisfaction or dissatisfaction as linked with chapter four. CRM technology is critical for customer experience analysis and strategy plans.

Both customer journeys and customer experience contribute to business performance because they are connected to revenue and profits and must always be prioritised for retaining a company's market position.

Chapter Seven

Digital Technology Transformation

Chapter Introduction

THIS CHAPTER SPECIFICALLY focuses on providing a high-level overview of digital technology. The main goal is to identify the distinct types of digital technology and how critical they are to designing customer journeys (processes) and customer experiences for online and offline channels. Here, we can see how this chapter is linked to chapter five on customer journeys and chapter six covering customer experiences.

Digital technology plays a significant role in operating model design across the business value chain facilitated by process mapping and process automation. Process mapping models can be used to analyse complex business problems and come up with digital technology to address those issues.

Chapter Learning Outcomes

The key learning objectives will include the following:

- Definition of digital technology.
- Technology innovation companies in 2020.
- Types of digital technology.

- How digital technology contributes to customer journey processes and the customer experience.
- How process mapping contributes to digital technology.
- How digital technology is linked to corporate strategy.

The chapter is intended to provide a holistic picture of how process mapping as a methodology integrated with digital technology can be used to come up with an architecture that meets customer requirements and overall customer satisfaction.

Defining Technology and Digital Transformation (DX)

Technology and digital transformation are the responsibilities of the IT department for implementation across the organisation. Digital technology is effectively a function within the IT department. The chief information officer (CIO) heads the IT department, including the execution of corporate strategy.

Digital transformation can be described as how an organisation uses digital technology to operate the business and deliver products and services to customers.

Salesforce defines digital transformation as "the process of using digital technologies to create new – or modify existing business processes, culture, and customer experiences to meet constantly changing businesses and market requirements." (*Source: Salesforce.com*)

"Digital transformation marks a radical rethinking of how an organisation uses technology, people, and processes to change business performance fundamentally," says George Westerman, MIT principal research scientist and author of *Leading Digital: Turning Technology into Business Transformation*.

"Ideally led by the CEO, in partnership with CIOs, Chief HR Officers (CHROs) and other senior leaders, digital transformation requires cross-departmental collaboration in pairing business-focused philosophies with rapid application development models." Such changes are undertaken to pursue new business models and new revenue streams and are driven by changes in customer expectations around products and services. Customer expectations are far exceeding what you can really do," says Westerman. "That means a fundamental rethinking about what we do with technology in organisations." (George Westerman, MIT principal research scientist and author of *Leading Digital: Turning Technology into Business Transformation*).

Technology Innovation Companies in 2020

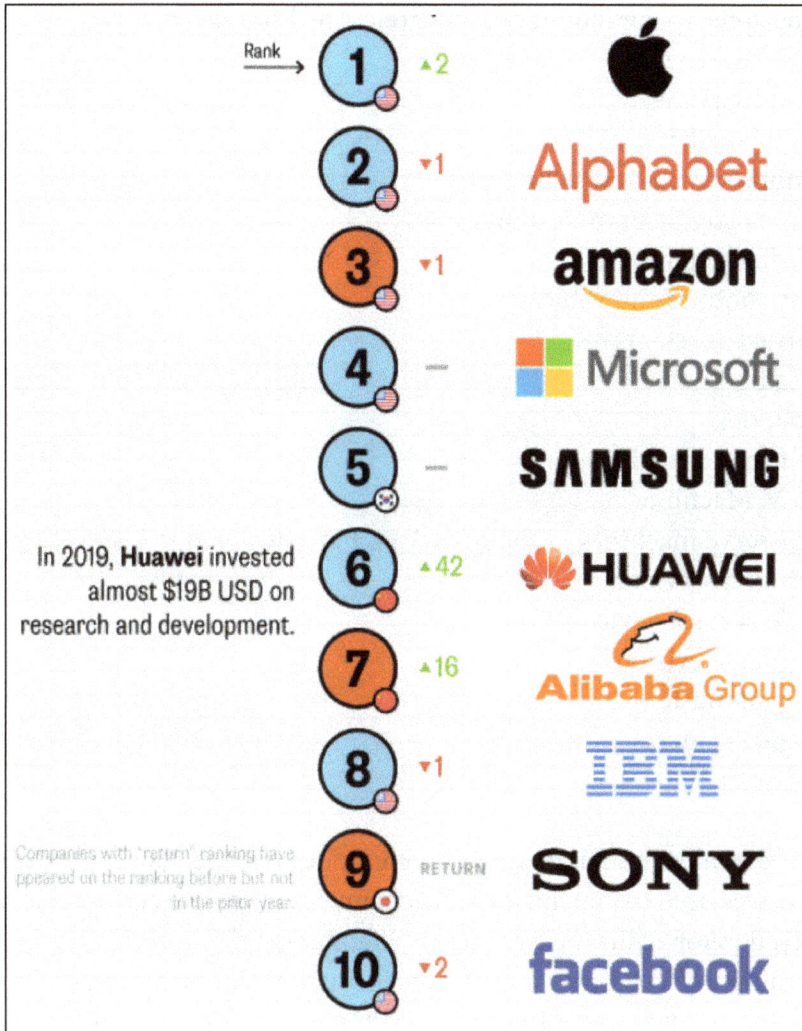

Figure 80: *Innovative Companies 2020 (Source: Visualcapitalist.com)*

A digital channel is a platform used to engage a targeted audience and the most widely deployed types of digital technology cover these areas:

- Websites
- Telephony or interactive voice recognition (IVR)
- Computers

- Cloud computing
- Smart mobile phones
- Smartphones for landlines and wireless technology
- Smartwatches
- Email services
- Social media
- Online buying and selling
- Search engine optimisation (SEO)
- Medical equipment
- Automobiles and vehicles
- Virtual assistants
- Chatbots
- Robotics
- Self-scan machines
- ATM Machines
- Self-serve machines in supermarkets and other industries
- Printing services
- Field service devices
- Digital television
- Digital music
- Digital cameras
- E-books

The list of digital technology categories continues but the above are examples of how businesses need to maximise digital channels to improve customer experience and satisfaction for achieving revenue growth, market share, and cost reduction.

According to *PWC.com*, "digital transformation can be accelerated by seamlessly combining the business strategy, customer experience, and technology to transform business and achieve durable growth."

This means that the digital strategy must be driven by the corporate strategy to ensure alignment between the two directions. The accounting firm has identified the main types of digital transformation which consist of the following components:

- Core enterprise processes
- Operating business models
- Customer experience
- Supply chain

The benefits of Digital Transformation and Process Improvement innovation, as obtained from *CIO-enterprise.com,* include the following:

- Cost reduction
- Improved customer experience
- Consolidated business operations and workflows
- Provision of extensive and accurate data analytics
- More customer-centric focus
- Increased market share through customer co-creating product design
- Creation of suitable marketing strategies
- Establishment of high-performing cultures
- Fostering cross-functional collaboration within the organisation

Benefits of Adopting a Digital Technology Model

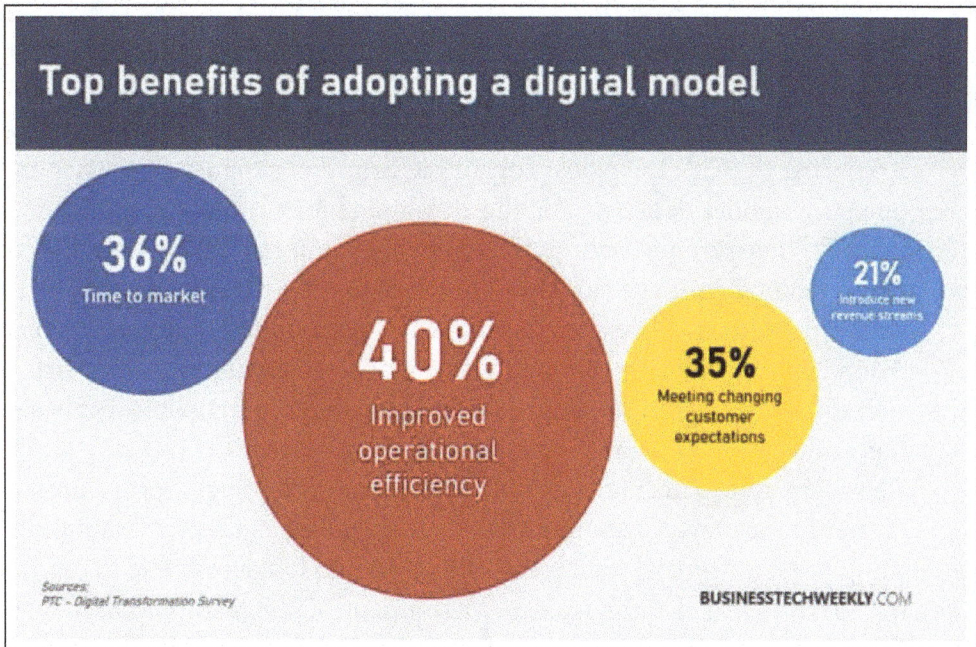

Figure 81: *Digital Model Post-COVID-19 (Source: BusinessTechWeekly.com)*

Digitisation Enhancing Customer Journeys and Customer Experience

Digital technology contributes to customer journey processes by creating digital customer journey processes. This is the total digital interactions your customers have with your brand's online and offline stores.

These interactions can be multiple, depending on the digital channels that the organisation provides to its customers through the purchasing journey both online and offline. This is where omnichannel retail is most effective. This is the term used to describe where customers are provided with the same customer service on the company's multiple digital channels that are integrated on all devices and platforms.

Digital technology is expected to provide a simplified, quicker, and more enjoyable customer journey process and experience.

In designing digital technology, here are some principles that contribute to customer journey processes generating positive customer satisfaction:

- Invest in the digital omnichannel approach to ensure that the brand is consistent with multiple digital platforms.
- Facilitate customer involvement to build a digital customer journey process. According to *BCG*, the global consulting firm that supports processes and operating model designs, "For the development of a successful customer journey strategy, organisations must reimagine internal processes, embrace new operating structures and modifications to old policies and procedures, and be ready to enhance current products and services." (*Source: BCG.com*)
- Adopting new digital technologies to enhance customer journey satisfaction such as process automation, artificial intelligence (AI), machine learning, and many other emerging technologies. (*Source: BCG.com*).
- Replacing legacy technology with advanced technology contributes to customer journey processes rather than spending significant amounts of funds to fix technology that is out of date and no longer suitable to cater to the current market and business environments. (*Source: BCG.com*).
- Personalise the digital customer journey process by helping organisations customise the experiences and content. A fine example is provided by Nike, which has multiple websites in different regions to cater to customers' unique needs.

- Obtain a competitive advantage, outperforming competitors through new customer acquisition and high retention rates. This enables the company to have a higher market share and more customers purchasing their products.

Digital Benchmarking with Competitors

The benchmarking in this section is between Primark and H&M, two highly recognisable clothing brands on the UK high street and global markets.

Both the clothing retailers are competitors, with H&M having a higher global presence providing both online and offline shopping channels.

H&M's operating model is like Primark's because they offer low prices for their clothing and other products, but their supply chains are exceptionally different.

Primark has not considered adopting online shopping, with their executive team and business strategy preferring offline shopping. (*Source: BBC.com*)

Primark and H&M Online Digital Benchmarking

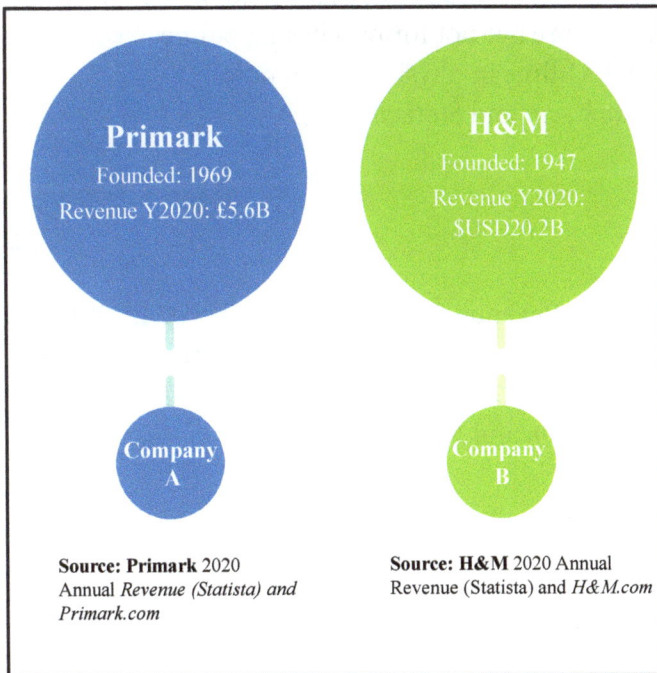

Primark
Founded: 1969
Revenue Y2020: £5.6B

H&M
Founded: 1947
Revenue Y2020: $USD20.2B

Company A

Company B

Source: Primark 2020 Annual *Revenue (Statista) and Primark.com*

Source: H&M 2020 Annual Revenue (Statista) and *H&M.com*

Figure 82: *Primark and H&M Benchmarking*

Some of the main reasons for opting out of the online shopping channel are associated with non-value-adding online processes, such as processing high refunds, which could impact overall profits and low prices offered to their customers.

Primark insists that the company is on a low margin and must be competitive on low price offerings. Going online is a significant financial challenge for the retailer because they would have to integrate their entire supply chain with operational systems to support online processes which warrant a significant capital expenditure.

Since 2020, when the pandemic started, Primark lost £1.05B during lockdown due to the halt in trading, both online and offline, as reported in January 2021.

The financial results saw a decline of 30% in revenue as of January 2021, while a 40% rise for Primark's competitor online retailers like ASOS and Boohoo, which rose in the last quarter of 2020. (*Source: BBC.com*)

Primark

Revenue: Annual Revenue, £5.6B 2020, £7.79B 2019
Digital Website: New website to be launched in 2022 to display more items available in the store but not for purchasing online
Sales Channel: Offline in physical stores only
Source: *Primark.com* and *Statista.com*

H&M

Revenue: Annual Revenue, USD20.2B 2020, USD24.3 2019
Digital Website: The website exists with customers purchasing online
Sales Channel: Offline and online purchasing
Source: *Primark.com* and *Statista.com*

How Digital Processes Contribute to Business Continuity

IT Strategy and Corporate Strategy

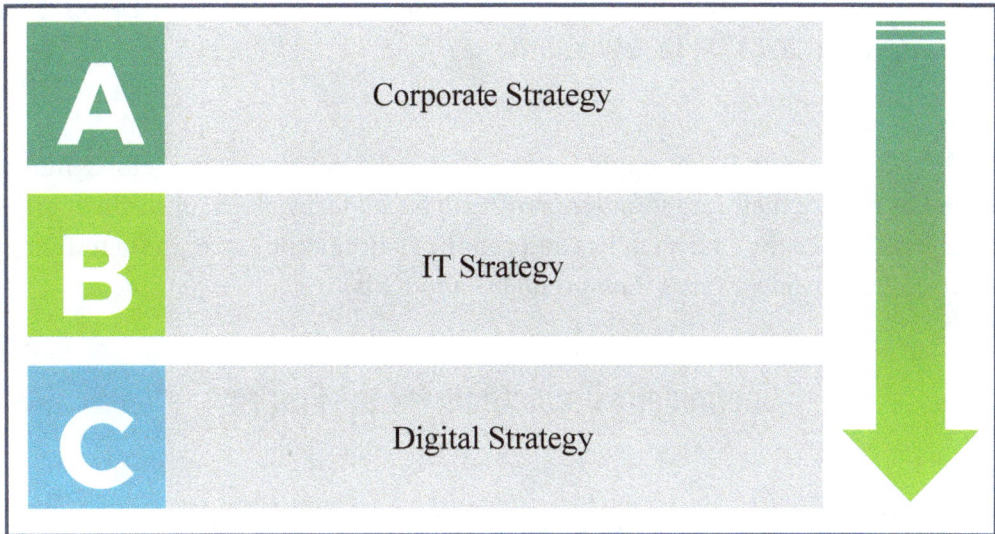

Figure 83: *Digital Strategy linked to Corporate Strategy*

Before creating a digital strategy that will link to the corporate strategy, *Salesforce* recommends the following steps (*Salesforce.com*):

- Knowing the customer audience.
- Reviewing and monitoring data analytics on current customer channels.
- Analysing the competitive landscape.
- Defining the digital strategy objectives and monitoring performance.

The objective of any digital strategy is to improve the customer experience and align with the corporate strategy to improve sales volume and market share. According to *Salesforce*, "by the end of 2017, two-thirds of the 2000 global companies will have digital transformation at the center of their corporate strategy." In 2021, with the COVID-19 pandemic crisis, this percentage is higher than was predicted in 2017.

Case Example

Digital Transformation Will Exceed 53% of IT budgets by 2023 (*Techrepublic.com – IDC: "Digital Transformation Spending Will Eat Up 53% of IT Budgets by 2023" – TechRepublic*)

The prediction from TechRepublic states that most businesses will either modernise or replace their legacy systems with advanced technology, implement artificial intelligence for data analytics and robotics automation, or align their digital metrics with business value measurements and KPIs.

Technology Predictions for the Future

Prediction 1 – Co-creation of Innovation with Customers

By 2022, customer collaboration and co-innovation will innovate customer journeys, customer experience, and satisfaction.

Prediction 2 – Artificial Intelligence Maximisation

AI is to be maximised in providing detailed information about customers and predicting customer behaviour to get ahead of competitors.

Prediction 3 – Digital offerings

By 2023, 50% of organisations that invest in digital innovation will increase their market share compared to those that choose not to invest.

Prediction 4 – AI and Digital Workforce

Last year, in 2021, there was a significant demand for AI and a digital workforce, creating new opportunities in existing and new markets.

Prediction 5 – Digital KPIs Mature

In 2020, they predicted a potential growth of 60% with companies eliminating their existing KPI metrics with revised metrics driven by digital metrics.

Prediction 6 – Replace Legacy Platforms

Companies will be investing in replacing legacy systems with innovative advanced technology and business process management that support their customer experience and customer satisfaction.

Prediction 7 – Invest in Business Intelligence

By 2023, organisations will invest in new intelligence technologies to enable their business to make informed decisions about their strategy, business operations, customer experience, and business architecture throughout the process of selling their products and services to customers.

It is noticeably clear from the predictions that becoming an HPO will require investment in digital technology through insights and advanced architecture to support the current and future state ecosystems.

Summary

Digital technology adaptation by many organisations has accelerated because of the COVID-19 pandemic. Most companies have effectively been forced to invest in digital channels such as the internet, artificial intelligence, process automation, and robotics for performance improvements.

This chapter has defined and provided examples of digital technology. The key message is that companies have to adapt to digital technology or lose their customers in the long term who can switch over to alternative retailers.

Chapter Eight

Growth and Profitability for Long-Term Success

Chapter Introduction

A LL BUSINESSES EXIST TO make a profit excluding non-profit organisations. This chapter shows how process mapping contributes to healthy profits through process improvement techniques that increase revenue and those specifically designed to reduce operational costs.

The profit equation has been specifically used to illustrate how process improvement methodologies add value to achieve those profit goals.

This chapter effectively connects all previous chapters in the book, from chapter one, which focuses on process architecture, to chapter two, concerning how to perform process mapping, all the way through to chapter three on risk management, chapter four on process improvement models, chapter five on customer journeys, chapter six on customer experience, and chapter seven on digital technology.

Chapter Learning Outcomes

The key learning objectives will include the following:

- Definition of profitability.
- How process mapping contributes to achieving profitability.

- How process mapping is linked to business growth.
- Why global companies like Amazon have enjoyed success by adopting process frameworks in their operating models and value chains.

The chapter is effectively consolidating all the other chapters to arrive at an equation that is supported by process mapping to achieve profitability.

Defining Profitability

Profitability is company revenue deducting costs to generate a positive return. This book demonstrates how business process maximisation reduces costs and increases company profitability over a projected time frame.

An example of how gross profits and revenue are increased while direct costs are reduced due to business process improvement techniques is illustrated below:

Profitability Equation

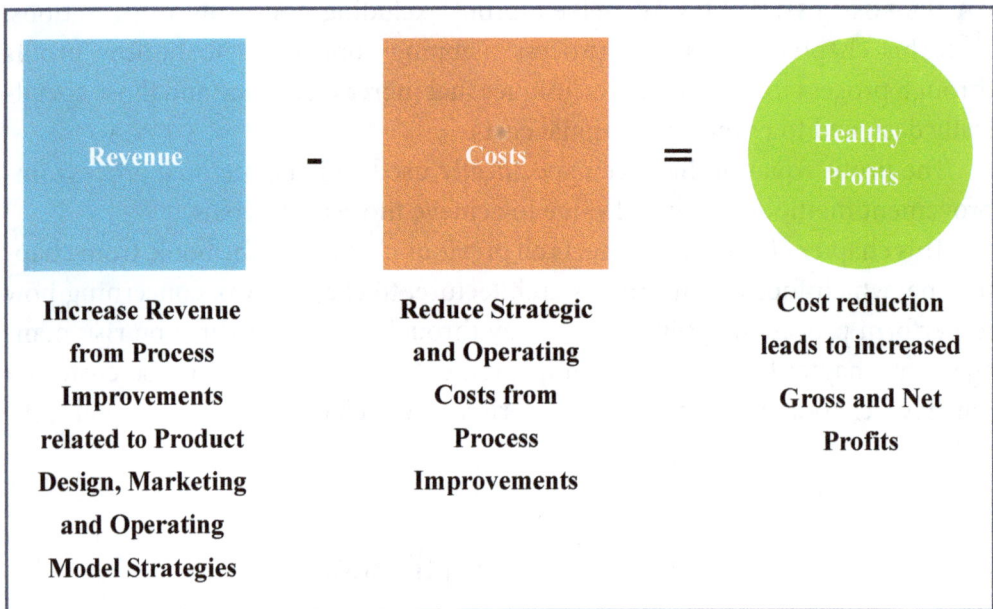

Revenue	-	Costs	=	Healthy Profits
Increase Revenue from Process Improvements related to Product Design, Marketing and Operating Model Strategies		Reduce Strategic and Operating Costs from Process Improvements		Cost reduction leads to increased Gross and Net Profits

Figure 84: *Profit Equation from Process Optimisation*

Any department or function that has had process re-engineering or process improvements will benefit from cost savings associated with efficiencies such as automation, standardisation, and elimination of non-value-adding activities.

How Process Mapping Contributes to Profitability

Process mapping contributes to maximising customer satisfaction mainly because customers will be happy with the service from their customer experience and product quality design. The goal here is that process mapping helps determine what's valuable to customers when designing customer journey processes and the overall customer experience. This, in effect, means that customers' retention and referral rates will be higher, with new customers being acquired at the same time.

This scenario was experienced during the pandemic when many customers turned to Amazon online retail for most of their purchases in 2020. Even though there were resource constraints during the COVID-19 era, Amazon still delivered outstanding services to its customers. As a result, its customer retention and new customer acquisition rates increased tremendously, contributing to the annual sales of 386 billion USD in 2020. (*Source: Statista.com*)

The process mapping improvement techniques have an impact on how your business is positioning its brand and performing against competitors. It starts with the corporate strategy for mapping processes and choosing to make customers the focal point of every business decision across all levels of the organisation.

Customer satisfaction is the result of process improvement in collaboration with customers' needs and wants to be addressed in product design and service.

Therefore, creating a culture within an organisation that prioritises customer needs and wants is fundamental for long-term success and growth.

Blockbuster ceased trading because the company did not prioritise customer experience, process design, and digital technology. Competitors, like Amazon and Netflix, entered the video store market in the 1990s, which inevitably improved customer experience and satisfaction levels, with customers not having to be inconvenienced by physically going to the stores to rent videos, as they were now able to watch movies from any location without leaving their homes.

The new customer experience and valuable product design offerings were significant factors that contributed to the decline of Blockbuster's market share.

This leads to the discussion of operational improvement, supply chain innovation, and productivity. Not only has customer satisfaction improved but the cycle times in delivering products and services also outperformed customer expectations.

Revenue Increasing Due to Positive Customer Satisfaction

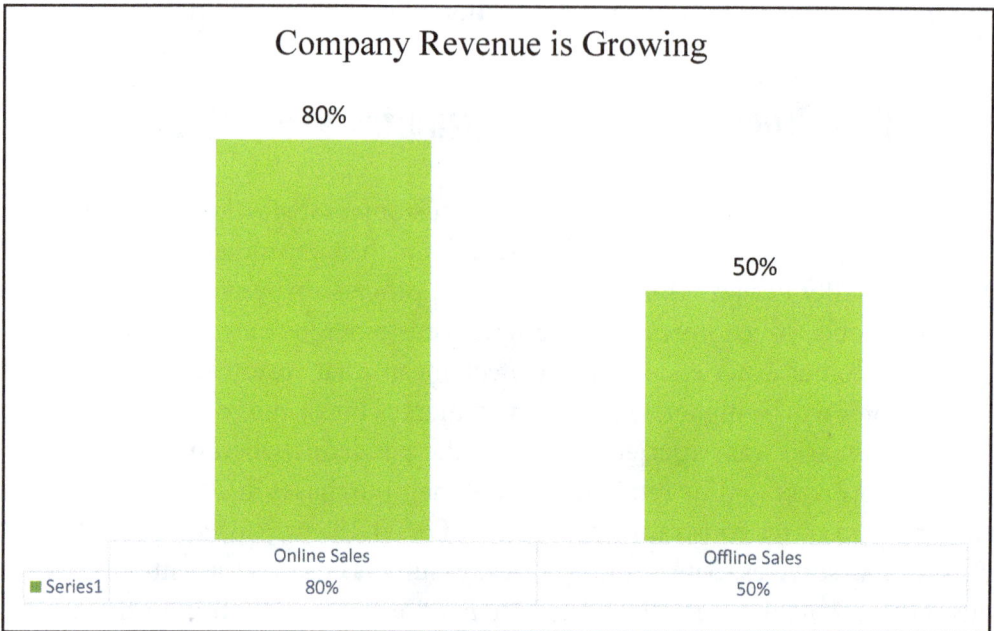

Company Revenue is Growing

80%

50%

	Online Sales	Offline Sales
■ Series1	80%	50%

Figure 85: *Sales Growth from Customer Satisfaction*

What will be obvious in the company's revenue increase or decline is revealed in the customer satisfaction metrics. The customer satisfaction metrics, like net promoter scoring (NPS), customer satisfaction score (CSAT), customer service satisfaction (CSS), customer reviews, and many others, show the correlation between revenue and customer satisfaction.

Where the customer metrics are high and positive, the revenue will be high as well, but where the customer metrics are low, there will be a decline in revenue.

How Process Mapping is Linked to Company Growth

Corporate growth strategies are usually associated with expansion (mergers and acquisitions), downsizing, or company improvement. The goal is to increase customer revenue from new customer acquisitions and retention of existing customers. Irrespective of the strategic choice, the company can only achieve maximum

Revenue Declining Due to Negative Customer Satisfaction

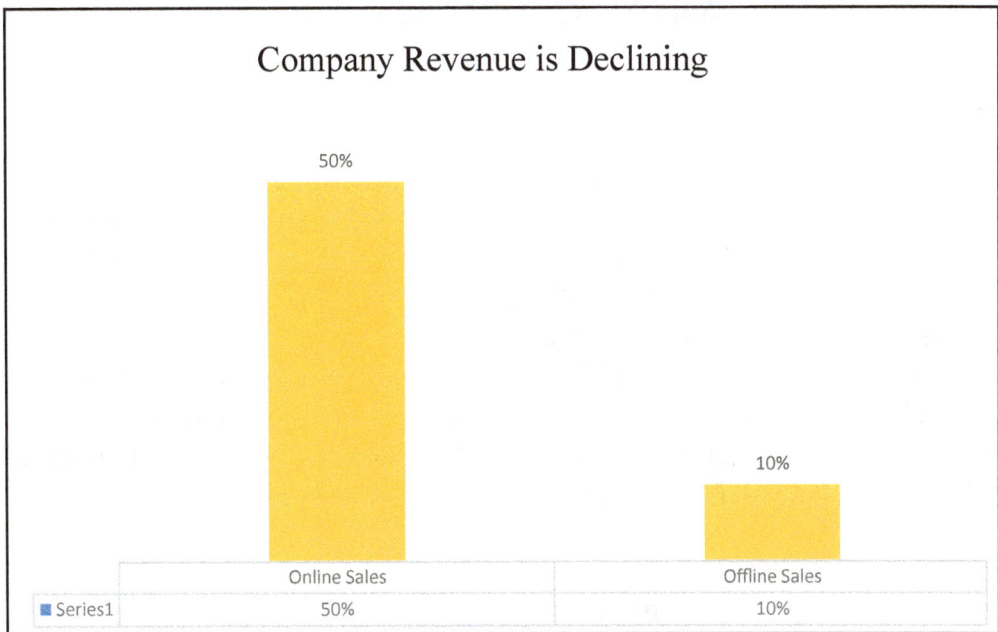

Company Revenue is Declining

	Online Sales	Offline Sales
■ Series1	50%	10%

Figure 86: *Sales Decline from Negative Customer Satisfaction*

performance where process re-engineering or improvement techniques have been applied. If process management is not performed, that company will not be able to derive maximum profits.

The four types of growth strategies include: (*Source: Corporatefinanceinstitute.com*)

- Market penetration: expanding in existing markets with existing products.
- Market development: entering a new market with new products.
- Product development: new products in existing markets.
- Diversification: new products in new markets.

Examples of successful companies that have transformed their processes through Six Sigma, Lean Six Sigma, or other methodologies to achieve global growth include Amazon and Apple.

Profitability Benchmarking between Competitors

(*Source: Washingtonpost.com*)

Apple and Samsung, two of the largest consumer electronics companies in the world, are being benchmarked for their quality of smartphones in relation to their business processes contributing to customer experience and satisfaction.

In 2016, when Galaxy 7 manufactured by Samsung was launched, there were incidents of the mobile phones catching fire and, in some cases, even exploding because of battery and product design issues.

The technical glitch of the Galaxy 7 model was a health and safety issue that resulted not only in customer dissatisfaction, but also raised questions about the compliance and regulatory requirements. Unsurprisingly, the fiscal impact resulted in a rapid loss of 26 billion USD on the stock market.

Profitability Benchmarking between Apple and Samsung

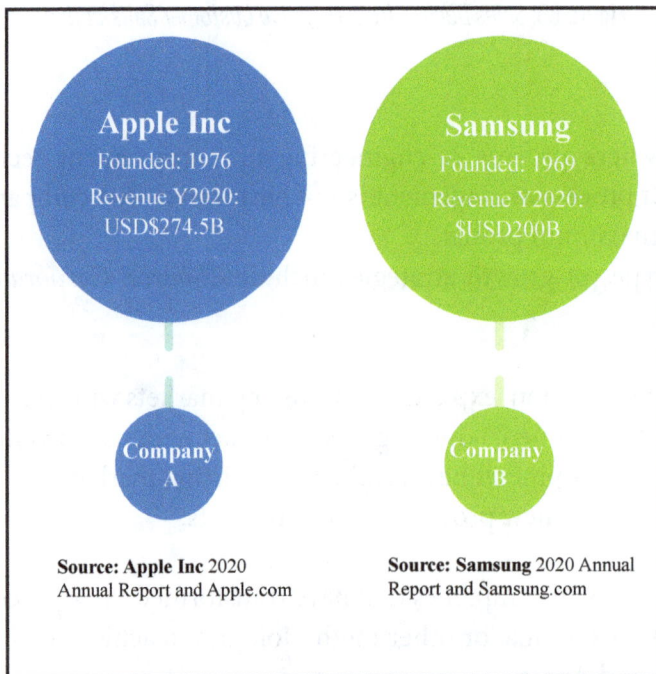

Figure 87: *Annual Revenues for Apple and Samsung*

It transpired that the root cause of the problem was connected to process quality control failures involving batteries being forced to fit into compartments that were too small to accommodate. The product recall cost Samsung 5.3 billion USD to gather the smartphones and re-test them for quality control and assurance.

Samsung Executives reviewed their complicated processes that involved the launching of new smartphones in the market to determine the root cause of the health and safety issues. Apple had its iPhone product recalled, but their health and safety defects were never as severe as those of the Galaxy 7 in 2016. This is mainly because Apple invests extensively on its supply-chain and outsourced development processes to mitigate the risk of product quality failures.

Apple

Annual Revenue: USD 274.5 billion
Product Recalls: iPhone 12 Pro hardware issue causing sound issues in 2021
Severity of the Product Recalls: Low
Source: *Apple.com*, *Statista.com*, and *Forbes.com*

Samsung

Annual Revenue: USD 200 billion
Product Recalls: 2.5 million smartphones recall for Galaxy 7, regarded as the largest smartphone recall in the world in 2016/2017
Severity of the Product Recalls: Exceptionally high
Source: *Samsung.com*, *Statista.com*, and *Washingtonpost.com*

How Profitability Contributes to Business Continuity

Process management makes a significant contribution to the success of a company in achieving short-term and long-term profits. The short-term profits are focused on the working capital and operational needs, while the long-term is centred on balance sheet risk management and other longer-term strategies. (*Prudential Private Capital*)

Process techniques are essential for improving financial performance measurements like identifying the right key performance indicators (KPIs) to measure, introducing automation to replace manual procedures, and providing easier access to data analytics for performing business intelligence reporting.

Benefits of short-term profits include the following:

- Generate liquid capital and cashflow to cover short-term current liabilities such as payments to suppliers, employees, interest rate repayments, and many others. Then provide multiple opportunities for short-term income obtained from financial and treasury investments.
- Build credit history for the company and ensure that credit rating is not affected, demonstrating sustainable liquidity and meeting obligations.
- Funding for marketing campaigns and product development to be used for generating future revenue and profitability for the company.

Profitability and Performance Management

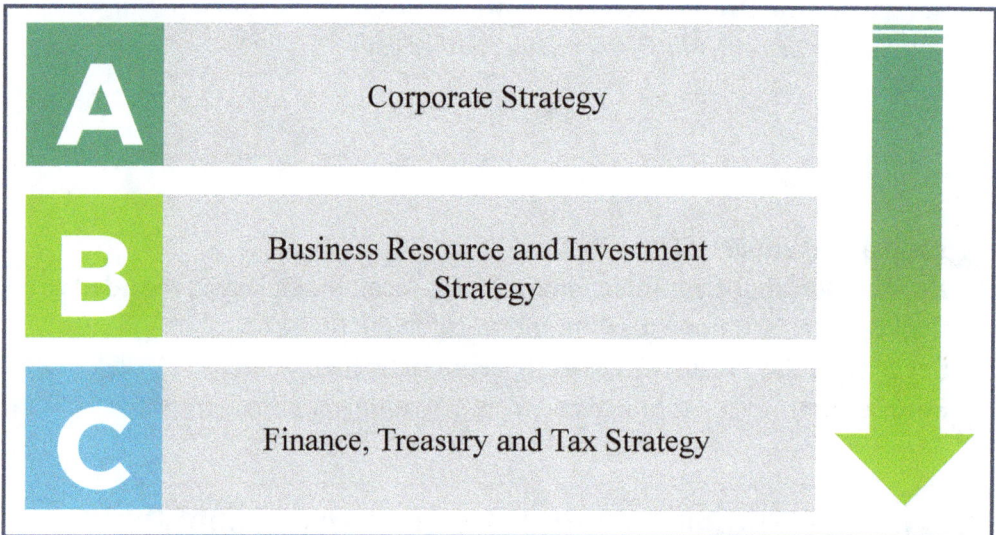

Figure 88: *Profitability defining the going concern of a business*

Benefits of long-term profits cover the following:

- Align with the corporate strategy and long-term financial goals to materialise their returns on investment based on that long-term vision.

- Growth plans which focus on financing the entire product portfolio for achieving market growth, market expansions, and profitability in the long-term.
- Improve investor relationships and performance measurements to ensure that positive ROI is achieved, or timelines given for achieving those financial commitments to the investors.
- If a company consistently makes losses resulting in a crunch of capital or resources essential for managing the company, then the future is at risk.

Case Example

Bain & Company, The Change Process Which Unlocked Potential and Profits (*Source: Bain.com*)

The consulting firm was hired to provide operational efficiency through process improvements, resource re-allocation, and organisational design for the credit division based in a European Bank.

Some of the major bottlenecks were caused by the staff performing non-value-adding activities because the operations were not aligned with the overall strategy and there were no robust systems to support the required activities.

Critical Problems

- Operating model consisted of outdated legacy systems.
- Misallocation of resources with staff spending a significant amount of time on non-customer-related activities.
- Poor organisation design that was not aligned with corporate strategy.
- Extensive longer decision-making processes due to lack of automated systems and reporting capability for providing real-time information.
- Lack of automated reporting software for business intelligence and KPI metrics and performance measurements.

- Credit processes not identified or documented to assist with work prioritisations and organisational structures.
- High operating costs in managing the credit division that impacted profits.

Achievements

- Profit improvement projections consisted of 17% profit improvement after year one and 147% profit improvement after the third year.
- Process redesign and re-engineering through documenting processes for the division, including the implementation of those processes.
- Streamlined credit processes for improving cycle times and KPI measures.
- Created a new organisational structure with a change management team consisting of a steering committee, implementation teams, and required personnel per region.
- Reallocated roles and responsibilities across multiple regions and branches.
- Developed new industry reporting tools to improve business intelligence and performance measurement.
- Introduced new system workflows or system processes for the credit division to achieve efficiencies.
- Customer segmentation to prioritise serving customers based on profitability.

Summary

This chapter shows that process improvement, as mentioned in the benchmarking and case example, reduces operational costs and increases profit margins.

The financial statistics of the bank from year one to year three demonstrate the value processes made in achieving performance measurements.

The Galaxy 7 smartphone incident that occurred at Samsung is a great illustration of process maps providing quality assurance in ensuring that specific tasks and decisions are followed. If specific processes and decisions are not followed, they can result in high operational costs involving product recalls, reworks, fines, and bad publicity.

Without process improvements, it is not possible to achieve high margins because customer expectation and satisfaction will be impacted, resulting in reduced revenue, higher costs, and lower profitability.

Conclusion

Pᴿᴼᶜᴱˢˢ ᴹᴬᴺᴬᴳᴱᴹᴱᴺᵀ ɪˢ ᴼᴺᴱ of the fundamental reasons why some companies are more competitive than others. The technique of documenting company activities to understand the current operations correctly and planning how the business will operate is critical for any business transformation.

Process management starts with the big-picture thinking about the company in the short-term, medium-term, and larger time frame. How a company can adapt quickly to the external environment is governed by how well its processes have been managed and measured for sustainable management and business growth.

Cost reduction in headcount and the organisational design are paramount to understanding the structure, technology, and processes underpinning the management of the business functions.

Below is a list of established global brands that employ Six Sigma and other process methodology techniques (*Source: 6Sigma.com and 6Sigma.us.com*)

- Apple
- Amazon
- Microsoft
- Coca-Cola
- Toyota
- Mercedes Benz
- McDonald's
- Walt Disney

Here, we see a correlation between companies that deploy process innovation and those that are regarded to be the world's most valuable brands, such as Apple, Amazon, Microsoft, Google, Coca-Cola, Toyota, and other retailers.

The World's Most Valuable Brands

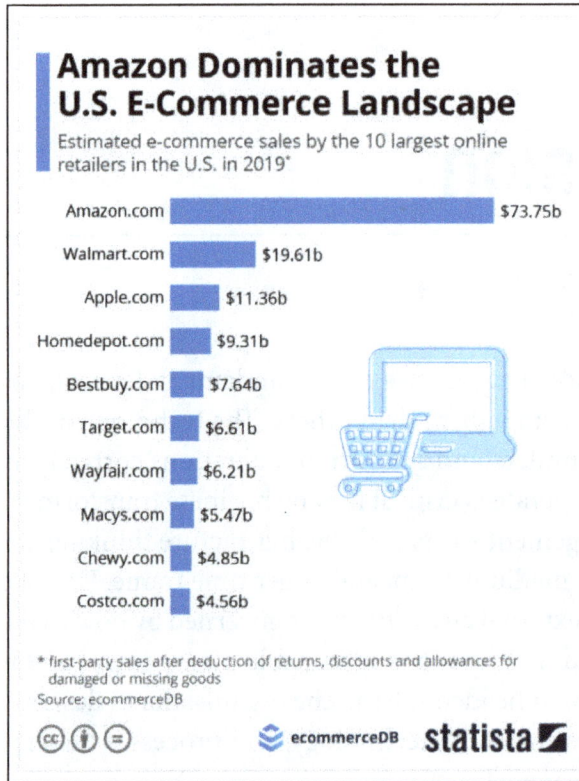

Amazon Dominates the U.S. E-Commerce Landscape

Estimated e-commerce sales by the 10 largest online retailers in the U.S. in 2019*

Amazon.com	$73.75b
Walmart.com	$19.61b
Apple.com	$11.36b
Homedepot.com	$9.31b
Bestbuy.com	$7.64b
Target.com	$6.61b
Wayfair.com	$6.21b
Macys.com	$5.47b
Chewy.com	$4.85b
Costco.com	$4.56b

* first-party sales after deduction of returns, discounts and allowances for damaged or missing goods
Source: ecommerceDB

ecommerceDB statista

Figure 89: *Worlds Valuable Brands 2020 (Source: Statista.com)*

The pre-COVID-19 economic environment has significantly changed the business landscape in how businesses deliver products and services to their customers.

Some fundamental reasons include customers becoming more knowledgeable and nurturing elevated expectations as regards customer experience and satisfaction. This is mainly because of social media and information readily available on the media channels.

The second reason involves the saturated competitive landscape with multiple sellers on platforms, such as Amazon, eBay, Shopify, Alibaba, and many others. This scenario gives customers the bargaining power to switch retailers and suppliers because they are provided with numerous options.

Then, there are unpredictable economic factors such as COVID-19, inflation, weather interruptions, and macro and micro fiscal policies at national and global levels. And lastly, process improvement from AI automation and digital optimisation is also a telling factor.

In performing a comparison study of how process mapping and innovation have contributed to significant growth and profitability, here are some examples from the globally recognisable brands:

Evidence of Process Improvement or Process Re-engineering and Project Results [2021] That Generated Extensive Cost Reduction and Improved Customer Satisfaction (*Source: Aimultiple.com*)

Business Name	Process Method	Process Software	Process Category	Process Benefit
Dell EMC	Robotic Process Automation	Automation anywhere	Various processes such as invoicing process, renewal quote generation	· $2M savings per year
Ernst and Young [EY]	Robotic Process Automation		Tickets booked for personal use	· 50% reduction in effort · 20% reduction in air travel ticket prices
Hewlett Packard [HP]	Robotic Process Automation	Uipath	Invoice tax accounting and reporting sub-processes automated	· 85% reduction in effort leading to $100k cost savings
Nokia	Robotic Process Automation		Order-to-Cash and Process-to-Pay	· Harmonization of different processes · Improved lead times
One of Big 4	Robotic Process Automation		Tax returns, business intelligence reporting	· $18m savings p.a.
A global pharmaceutical company	Business Process Management	Flowforma	Artwork management	· 60% efficiency improvement · Full visibility of the entire process · Increased coordination with other departments in different countries
A US regulatory body	Business Process Management		Quality management	· Reduced cycle time by 50% · Increased process throughput by 40% · Improved quality

Figure 90: *Profitability from Process Improvements*

Work performed in a company that eliminates manual procedures and replaces those with robust automated processes is a key driver for long-term growth and sustainable profitability right now and in the future.

It is also important to stress how operational excellence needs to be supported by the board and executive team to achieve successful process implementation.

And this is the reason companies like Apple, Amazon, Microsoft, Google, McDonald's Coca-Cola, Mercedes Benz, and others are consistently outperforming their competitors and have a significant market share in their sectors.

References

Introduction

1. https://performancedriver.wordpress.com/2010/05/19/typical-characteristics-of-a-high-performing-organization-banking/
2. Company Culture: What Is It? (thebalancecareers.com), https://www.thebalancecareers.com/what-is-company-culture-2062000
3. Company Culture Is Everyone's Responsibility (hbr.org), https://hbr.org/2021/02/company-culture-is-everyones-responsibility
4. Business culture definition and business etiquette tips, https://businessculture.org/business-culture/
5. The Balanced Scorecard – Simple explanation (supplychaintoday.com), https://www.supplychaintoday.com/the-balanced-scorecard-simple-explanation/
6. Defining Company Culture: It's About Business Performance, Not Free Meals And Game Rooms (forbes.com), https://www.forbes.com/sites/forbeshumanresourcescouncil/2019/01/15/defining-company-culture-its-about-business-performance-not-free-meals-and-game-rooms/?sh=dc925b21e9de
7. What is a project management office (PMO) and do you need one? (cio.com), https://www.cio.com/article/267012/what-is-a-project-management-office-pmo-and-do-you-need-one.html
8. Marketing Theories – Balanced Scorecard (professionalacademy.com), https://www.professionalacademy.com/blogs/marketing-theories-balanced-scorecard/

9. The Balanced Scorecard – Measures that Drive Performance (hbr.org), https://hbr.org/1992/01/the-balanced-scorecard-measures-that-drive-performance-2
10. The Moving Assembly Line (ford.com), https://corporate.ford.com/articles/history/moving-assembly-line.html

Chapter One: Business Process Strategy and Architecture Setup

1. Business Growth Strategy Consulting | BCG, https://www.bcg.com/capabilities/corporate-finance-strategy/business-strategy
2. The Standard Process Model meets SolMan 7.2 Process Management | SAP Blogs, https://blogs.sap.com/2017/01/20/the-standard-process-model-meets-solman-7.2-process-management/
3. Business Functions – PwC UK, https://www.pwc.co.uk/services/consulting/technology/business-functions.html
4. Industries | McKinsey & Company, https://www.mckinsey.com/industries
5. Statista Industry Overview, https://www.statista.com/markets/
6. bpm-overview.pdf (pwc.com), https://www.pwc.com/sk/en/bpm-cee/assets/bpm-overview.pdf
7. About the Business Process Model And Notation Specification Version 2.0 (omg.org), https://www.omg.org/spec/BPMN/2.0/
8. Microsoft Visio | Create Flowcharts & Diagrams in Visio, https://www.microsoft.com/en-gb/microsoft-365/visio/flowchart-software
9. Escaping the Doom Loop in Contact Center Operations | Bain & Company, https://www.bain.com/insights/escaping-the-doom-loop-in-contact-center-operations/
10. Oracle White Paper, https://www.oracle.com/us/products/applications/cx-metrics-kpi-dictionary-1966465.pdf
11. Why AI and Business Process Automation Share a Bright Future (cmswire.com), https://www.cmswire.com/digital-workplace/why-ai-and-business-process-automation-share-a-bright-future/
12. https://www.statista.com/statistics/266462/burger-king-revenue/
13. https://www.statista.com/statistics/219453/revenue-of-the-mcdonalds-corporation-by-geographic-region/
14. https://www.annualreports.com/Company/mcdonalds-corporation

15. Burger King | Investor Relations – Results Center (riweb.com.br), http://burgerking.riweb.com.br/listresultados.aspx?idCanal=BJOdwr7Mh2zM/7GDLBLQbQ

16. NYSE_MCD_2020.pdf (annualreports.com), https://www.annualreports.com/HostedData/AnnualReports/PDF/NYSE_MCD_2020.pdf

17. Burger King | Investor Relations – Results Center, ibid.

18. https://www.bdo.co.uk/en-gb/news/2019/british-businesses-commit-to-long-term-investment-in-automation

Chapter Two: Defining Business Process Mapping

1. Business Process Definition (appian.com), https://appian.com/bpm/business-process-definition.html

2. Definition of Business Process Management (BPM) – IT Glossary | Gartner, https://www.gartner.com/en/information-technology/glossary/business-process-management-bpm

3. Business process flows overview – Power Automate | Microsoft Docs, https://docs.microsoft.com/en-us/power-automate/business-process-flows-overview

4. Four ways to make better strategy choices | McKinsey, https://www.mckinsey.com/business-functions/strategy-and-corporate-finance/our-insights/seeing-your-way-to-better-strategy

5. Corporate Strategy – Corporate Strategy Consulting | BCG, https://www.bcg.com/capabilities/corporate-finance-strategy/corporate-strategy

6. https://corporatefinanceinstitute.com/resources/knowledge/strategy/corporate-strategy/

7. https://corporatefinanceinstitute.com/resources/knowledge/strategy/swot-analysis/

8. What Is the Growth Share Matrix? | BCG, https://www.bcg.com/en-gb/about/overview/our-history/growth-share-matrix

9. Strategy Evaluation SFA-analysis – JOHNSOHN.dk, https://johnsohn.dk/2019/08/03/strategy-evaluation-sfa-analysis/

10. Enduring Ideas: The 7-S Framework | McKinsey, https://www.mckinsey.com/business-functions/strategy-and-corporate-finance/our-insights/enduring-ideas-the-7-s-framework

11. Have you tested your strategy lately? | McKinsey, https://www.mckinsey.com/business-functions/strategy-and-corporate-finance/our-insights/have-you-tested-your-strategy-lately

12. Planning in an agile organization | McKinsey, https://www.mckinsey.com/business-functions/mckinsey-digital/our-insights/planning-in-an-agile-organization

13. The Standard Process Model meets SolMan 7.2 Process Management | SAP Blogs, https://blogs.sap.com/2017/01/20/the-standard-process-model-meets-solman-7.2-process-management/

14. What is an Action Priority Matrix? | Definition and Overview (productplan.com), https://www.productplan.com/glossary/action-priority-matrix/

15. https://corporatefinanceinstitute.com/resources/knowledge/strategy/swot-analysis/

16. The RACI matrix: Your blueprint for project success (cio.com), https://www.cio.com/article/287088/project-management-how-to-design-a-successful-raci-project-plan.html

17. ARIS loves Six Sigma | ARIS BPM Community (ariscommunity.com), https://www.ariscommunity.com/users/eva-klein/2010-01-22-aris-loves-six-sigma

18. http://www.aris.com/

19. https://camunda.com/

20. The Need to Reinvent Your Operating Models in a Post COVID World – Carpedia, https://carpedia.com/blog/the-need-to-reinvent-your-operating-models-in-a-post-covid-world/

21. The 30 retailers and restaurant chains that filed for bankruptcy in 2020 – CNN, https://edition.cnn.com/2020/12/12/business/retailers-restaurants-bankrupt-2020/index.html

22. Mercedes-Benz Guide to Electric Vehicles, https://www.mercedes-benz.co.uk/passengercars/mercedes-benz-cars/electric-vehicles/electric-vehicles.html

23. Mercedes-Benz History, https://www.mercedes-benz.com/en/classic/history/

24. Mercedes emergency call bug: Carmaker recalls vehicles – BBC News, https://www.bbc.co.uk/news/technology-56071108

25. Mercedes-Benz Production Factory Locations – Star Motor Cars, https://mercedesbenz.starmotorcars.com/blog/mercedes-benz-production-factory-locations/

26. Daimler Annual Report 2020, https://www.daimler.com/documents/investors/reports/annual-report/daimler/daimler-ir-annual-report-2020-incl-combined-management-report-daimler-ag.pdf
27. https://www.mercedes-benz.com/en/innovation/automotive-innovations-award-2020/
28. https://www.telegraph.co.uk/cars/news/tesla-model-3-takes-uk-car-year-title/
29. The Secret Of Tesla's Success Is Not Selling Cars: It's Being Able To Anticipate The Future (forbes.com), https://www.forbes.com/sites/enriquedans/2019/09/09/the-secret-of-teslas-success-is-not-selling-cars-its-being-able-to-anticipate-thefuture/?sh=73ee14904973
30. Electric Cars, Solar & Clean Energy | Tesla, https://www.tesla.com/
31. https://www.bbc.co.uk/news/technology-55902779
32. https://www.bmwgroup.com/content/dam/grpw/websites/bmwgroup_com/ir/downloads/en/2020/hauptversammlung/BMW-Group-Annual-Report-2019.pdf
33. https://www.press.bmwgroup.com/global/article/detail/T0322712EN/success-in-2020:-bmw-wins-numerous-titles-and-awards?language=en
34. https://www.bmwofreading.com/bmw-fuel-options/
35. https://camunda.com/wp-content/uploads/2021/10/Camunda-CaseStudy_Vodafone_EN.pdf

Chapter Three: Internal Controls and Risks of Business Processes

1. https://doi.org/10.1002/9781118691656.ch15
2. Another framework: COSO ERM. (2013). *Executive's Guide to COSO Internal Controls*, pp. 217-241. https://doi.org/10.1002/9781118691656.ch15
3. coso_table.png (859×514) (wsj.com), https://deloitte.wsj.com/riskandcompliance/files/2013/06/coso_table.png
4. Internal controls | ACCA Qualification | Students | ACCA Global, https://www.accaglobal.com/ca/en/student/exam-support-resources/fundamentals-exams-study-resources/f1/technical-articles/internal-controls.html
5. https://reciprocitylabs.com/resources/what-are-the-3-types-of-internal-controls/

6. Annual reports – Credit Suisse (credit-suisse.com), https://www.credit-suisse.com/about-us/en/reports-research/annual-reports.html

7. https://www.credit-suisse.com/media/assets/corporate/docs/about-us/investor-relations/financial-disclosures/financial-reports/csg-ar-2020-en.pdf

8. https://www.hsbc.com/-/files/hsbc/investors/hsbc-results/2020/annual/pdfs/hsbc-holdings-plc/210223-annual-report-and-accounts-2020.pdf?download=1

9. 2021 fines | FCA, https://www.fca.org.uk/news/news-stories/2021-fines

10. https://investors.natwestgroup.com/~/media/Files/R/RBS-IR-V2/results-center/19022021/natwest-group-announcement-fy2020.pdf

11. https://www.riskmanagementmonitor.com/risk-management-and-business-continuity-improving-business-resiliency/

12. https://www.protiviti.com/UK-en/business-continuity-management

13. Reciprocitylabs (2021). What are the three types of internal control. Available at: https://reciprocitylabs.com/resources/what-are-the-3-types-of-internal-controls/

14. https://www.investopedia.com/updates/enron-scandal-summary/

Chapter Four: Business Process Improvement Models

1. Coggin, K. (2018). "Waste Dispositioning process improvement project," https://doi.org/10.2172/1478632

2. Akintoye, A., Goulding, J. S.; Zawdie, G. (2012.). *Business Process Improvement*, Hoboken, NJ: Wiley-Blackwell. https://onlinelibrary.wiley.com/doi/book/10.1002/9781118280294

3. DMAIC | ARIS BPM Community (ariscommunity.com), https://www.ariscommunity.com/dmaic

4. DMAIC and DMADV Lenses to Examine Business Process | Process Exam | Process Exam, https://www.processexam.com/blog/dmaic-and-dmadv-lenses-examine-business-process

5. https://doi.org/10.2172/1478632

6. What is Six Sigma? Streamlining quality management (cio.com), https://www.cio.com/article/227977/six-sigma-quality-management-methodology.html

7. Toyota Production System | Vision & Philosophy | Company | Toyota Motor Corporation Official Global Website, https://global.toyota/en/company/vision-and-philosophy/production-system/

8. Womack, J. P., & Jones, D. T. (1996). *Lean Thinking: Banish Waste and Create Wealth in Your Corporation.* London: Simon & Schuster, 1996, p. 10.

9. https://www.leanproduction.com/

10. Lean And Six Sigma – A General Introduction | ARIS BPM Community (ariscommunity.com), https://www.ariscommunity.com/users/sixsigma/2012-03-14-lean-and-six-sigma-general-introduction

11. Theory of Constraints (TOC) | Lean Production, https://www.leanproduction.com/theory-of-constraints/

12. IAG – International Airlines Group – Results and reports (iairgroup.com), https://www.iairgroup.com/en/investors-and-shareholders/results-and-reports

13. https://skytraxratings.com/airlines/british-airways-rating

14. British Airways | Awards, https://mediacentre.britishairways.com/awards

15. https://skytraxratings.com/airlines/virgin-atlantic-rating

16. https://www.virgin.com/about-virgin/timeline

17. https://www.statista.com/statistics/309373/virgin-atlantics-uk-passenger-numbers/

18. Virgin Atlantic Annual Report 2019, https://flywith.virginatlantic.com/content/dam/corporate/Virgin%20Atlantic%20Annual%20Report%202019_Final.pdf

19. https://corporate.virginatlantic.com/gb/en/awards.html

20. https://skytraxratings.com/airlines/american-airlines-rating

21. https://news.aa.com/news/news-details/2020/American-Airlines-Group-Reports-Fourth-Quarter-and-Full-Year-2019-Profit-CORP-FI/default.aspx

22. Financial AAL | American Airlines (gcs-web.com), https://americanairlines.gcs-web.com/financial-results/financial-aal

23. https://research.aimultiple.com/process-improvement-case-studies/

Chapter Five: Customer Journey Mapping Techniques

1. Customer Journey Mapping | Microsoft Dynamics 365, https://dynamics.microsoft.com/en-gb/marketing/what-is-customer-journey-mapping/

2. Facebook quietly acquired another UK AI start-up and almost no one noticed | TechCrunch, https://techcrunch.com/2020/02/10/facebook-quietly-acquired-atlast-ml/

3. Nike buys an AI start-up that predicts what consumers want | TechCrunch, https://techcrunch.com/2019/08/07/nike-buys-an-ai-startup-that-predicts-what-consumers-want/

4. Sources: Amazon quietly acquired AI security start-up harvest.ai for around $20M | TechCrunch, https://techcrunch.com/2017/01/09/amazon-aws-harvest-ai/

5. Microsoft is buying AI start-up, Bonsai | TechCrunch, https://techcrunch.com/2018/06/20/microsoft-is-buying-a-ai-startup-bonsai/

6. https://oddballmarketing.com.au/blog/covid-19-changes-customer-journey/

7. https://investors.ebayinc.com/financial-information/annual-reports/default.aspx

8. Global paid Amazon Prime members 2020 | Statista, https://www.statista.com/statistics/829113/number-of-paying-amazon-prime-members/

9. https://www.statista.com/statistics/507881/ebays-annual-net-revenue/

10. https://www.forbes.com/sites/quora/2014/06/03/what-was-ebays-route-to-the-top/

11. NASDAQ_AMZN_2020.pdf (annualreports.com), https://www.annualreports.com/HostedData/AnnualReports/PDF/NASDAQ_AMZN_2020.pdf

12. https://www.statista.com/topics/846/amazon/

13. https://www.businessinsider.com/the-rise-and-fall-of-blockbuster-video-streaming-2020-1

Chapter Six: Redefining the Customer Experience

1. Transformation: the journey to customer-centricity (2015). *Customer Genius*, pp. 346-363. https://doi.org/10.1002/9781906465575.ch18

2. Customer experience strategy: Building a customer experience organization (2015). *Customer-Centric Marketing*, pp. 71-84. https://doi.org/10.1002/9781119154785.ch06

3. Walden, S. (2017). "Customer experience bad. Customer Experience Management Rebooted," pp. 207-216. https://doi.org/10.1057/978-1-349-94905-2_12

4. https://www.statista.com/chart/14043/top-10-online-stores-in-the-us/
5. Lafrenière, D. (2019). "Why is customer experience so important? Delivering Fantastic Customer Experience," pp. 5-14. https://doi.org/10.4324/9780429328091
6. https://techcrunch.com/2019/08/07/nike-buys-an-ai-startup-that-predicts-what-consumers-want/
7. https://www.statista.com/statistics/685734/nike-ad-spend/
8. Footwear News Achievement Awards 2020 Winners Revealed – Footwear News, https://footwearnews.com/2020/business/awards/fn-2020-achievement-award-winners-1203070085/
9. NIKE, Inc. – Investor Relations – Investors – News, Events and Reports, https://investors.nike.com/investors/news-events-and-reports/default.aspx
10. https://www.salesforce.com/blog/ai-boosts-adidas-personalized-email-marketing/
11. https://www.statista.com/statistics/540836/adidas-marketing-spend/
12. https://www.sportindustry.biz/sia/2020/winners
13. https://report.adidas-group.com/2020/en/
14. https://www.expertmarket.co.uk/crm-systems/amazon-crm-case-study

Chapter Seven: Digital Technology Transformation

1. How to Plan Your Digital Marketing Strategy – Salesforce Canada Blog, https://www.salesforce.com/ca/blog/2019/05/plan-digital-marketing-strategy.html
2. Accelerate Digital Transformation – Consulting – PwC UK, https://www.pwc.co.uk/services/consulting/accelerate-digital.html
3. What is Digital Transformation? A Definition by Salesforce, https://www.salesforce.com/products/platform/what-is-digital-transformation/
4. https://www.businesstechweekly.com/operational-efficiency/digital-transformation/guide-to-digital-transformation-for-smes/
5. https://www.bcg.com/capabilities/digital-technology-data/customer-journey
6. The 10 key benefits of digital transformation – Enterprise CIO News, https://www.enterprise-cio.com/news/2017/jun/26/10-benefits-of-digital-transformation/
7. https://www.bbc.co.uk/news/business-55661741
8. https://www.bbc.com/news/business-55661741

9. https://www.statista.com/statistics/252190/gross-sales-of-the-h-und-m-group-worldwide/
10. https://www.statista.com/statistics/383785/primark-revenue-worldwide/
11. https://find-and-update.company-information.service.gov.uk/company/00453448/filing-history
12. https://hmgroup.com/wp-content/uploads/2021/04/HM-Annual-Report-2020.pdf

Chapter Eight: Growth and Profitability for Long Term Sustainable Success

1. Amazon.com Inc. Available at: www.amazonAnnualReports.com
2. https://corporatefinanceinstitute.com/resources/knowledge/strategy/ansoff-matrix/
3. https://www.washingtonpost.com/business/how-samsung-moved-beyond-its-exploding-phones/2018/02/23/5675632c-182f-11e8-b681-2d4d462a1921_story.html
4. https://www.foxbusiness.com/technology/where-does-apple-make-iphones
5. https://investor.apple.com/investor-relations/default.aspx
6. https://www.samsung.com/global/ir/
7. https://www.statista.com/statistics/265125/total-net-sales-of-apple-since-2004/
8. https://www.statista.com/statistics/236607/global-revenue-of-samsung-electronics-since-2005/
9. Amazon – statistics & facts | Statista, https://www.statista.com/topics/846/amazon/
10. https://www.forbes.com/sites/gordonkelly/2021/11/24/apple-warning-iphone-hardware-problem-audio-recall-iphone-free-repair/
11. https://www.bain.com/client-results/change-process-unlocks-potential-and-profits/

Conclusion

1. https://research.aimultiple.com/process-improvement-case-studies/
2. 6Sigma.com
3. 6Sigma.us.com